WEEKENDS FOR TWO IN **NORTHERN CALIFORNIA**

BILL GLEESON | PHOTOGRAPHS BY JOHN SWAIN

weekends for two

IN
NORTHERN CALIFORNIA

FOURTH EDITION • COMPLETELY REVISED AND UPDATED

50 ROMANTIC GETAWAYS

CHRONICLE BOOKS
SAN FRANCISCO

ACKNOWLEDGMENTS

The author and photographer wish to thank the following people for their contributions, inspiration, and support:

Regina Miesch, photographic styling

Yvonne Gleeson, research assistance

Library of Congress Cataloging-in-Publication Data:

Gleeson, Bill.
  Weekends for two in northern California : 50 romantic
getaways / by Bill Gleeson ; photographs by John
Swain.—4th ed., completely rev. and updated.
      p. cm.
  Includes index.
  ISBN 0-8118-4003-4 (pbk.)
  1. Hotels—California, Northern—Guidebooks.
  2. Couples—Travel—California, Northern—Guidebooks.
  3. California, Northern—Guidebooks. I. Title.
  TX907.3.C2.G54 2004
  917.94'106154–dc22

                                    2004005723

Manufactured in China
Designed and typeset by Deborah Bowman
Prop styling by Regina Miesch

Distributed in Canada by Raincoast Books
9050 Shaughnessy Street
Vancouver, British Columbia V6P 6E5

10 9 8 7 6 5 4 3 2 1

Chronicle Books LLC
85 Second Street
San Francisco, California 94105

www.chroniclebooks.com

Table of Contents

THE WINE COUNTRY

SAN FRANCISCO AND THE BAY AREA

THE CENTRAL COAST

THE MOTHER LODE, SACRAMENTO, AND SIERRA

Introduction

Can it be that more than a decade has passed since we assembled the first volume of *Weekends for Two in Northern California*? Ten years, tens of thousands of miles, and tens of thousands of sold copies later, we're back with new destinations, all-new photography, and reports on revisits to many classic Northern California hideaways that helped make this book a best-seller when it was first introduced.

In those younger days, the combined pressures of work and children's activities made private time as a couple all too rare for us, the time between getaways measured in months, sometimes even seasons.

Today the nest is more or less empty and the two of us have more opportunities to indulge in time away. However, whether a weekend for two comes once a month or once a year, it's nothing to take lightly. We continue to approach each sojourn with a strategy that many might reserve for a round-the-world tour: maps, brochures, guidebooks, restaurant reviews, and itineraries. The only pieces absent from our strategy these days are the babysitter arrangements.

This book—as well as the others in the *Weekends for Two* series—is for couples like us: those who wish to minimize the element of chance that can cloud a cherished weekend for two and to do all they can to ensure that this special time away together lives up to expectations.

ROOMS FOR ROMANCE

After visiting hundreds of inns and small hotels across the country, we've honed our romantic criteria. Our checklist includes:

- Private bathrooms, a must in our opinion. We'll tell you if any are shared.
- In-room fireplaces. The warmth and glow of a fire is a natural complement to romance.
- Tubs or showers big enough for two—because a bathroom can be a romantic destination unto itself.
- Breakfast in bed or in your room. Many traveling romantics don't enjoy sharing a communal table with strangers.
- Canopied, four-poster king- or queen-sized beds and cushy comforters. Need we say why?
- Private decks, patios, or balconies with stimulating views. Most of us enjoy the inspiration of the outdoors.
- Comfortable couches, chaises, or love seats. The bed shouldn't be the only piece of furniture where two can be together.
- Rooms where smoking is not permitted. For many of us, nothing is more unromantic than a stale smoke smell.

We also seek out hotels and inns that exude that overall, sometimes difficult-to-describe intimate atmosphere and those that discourage child guests. Although we certainly harbor no prejudice toward children, having two of our own, we know that many couples are seeking a well-deserved break from the kids. The (sometimes loud) evidence of little people in the room next door or in the hall doesn't exactly contribute to a passionate getaway.

Finally, most inns and small hotels have certain special rooms that are particularly conducive to a romantic experience. Instead of leaving the choice of rooms to the innkeeper or her assistant and describing at length the public areas of each establishment, we've devoted a good part of this book to detailing particularly romantic rooms and suites. When booking your getaway reservation, don't hesitate to ask about the availability of one of these specific rooms—unless, of course, you already have a personal favorite.

DINING

At the beginning of each section, we've identified particularly noteworthy restaurants near our featured destinations. These were sampled by us and/or recommended by innkeepers whose opinions we respect. Keep in mind, however, that restaurants—and chefs—come and go. Accordingly, we suggest you balance these recommendations with updates and new choices offered by your innkeeper. In our experience, innkeepers are better than guidebooks as sources of up to date dining recommendations.

A WORD ABOUT RATES

While seasoned travelers may still be able to find a room along California's well-traveled highways for a song, this isn't a bargain hunter's guide. Since romantic getaways are special occasions, we've learned to adjust to the higher tariffs commanded for special rooms. In fact, most of the rooms described in the following pages start at more than $200 per night.

To help you plan your getaway budget, approximate 2005 rate ranges for specific rooms accompany each description. If you're booking a weekend trip, please note that many establishments require two-night minimum stays.

Rates (per high-season weekend night for two friendly people) are classified at the end of each listing using the following ranges, not including tax:

Moderate: Under $200
Expensive: $200–$300
Deluxe: Over $300

DAYTIME DIVERSIONS

If your legs are up to it, hike down the more than four hundred steps to the Point Reyes Lighthouse at the NATIONAL SEASHORE. It's a great place to snuggle against the wind and watch passing whales some three hundred feet below.

Twelve miles north of JENNER, and definitely worth a visit, is Fort Ross State Historic Park, a reconstructed fortress established by Russian seal hunters in the early 1800s. A little farther north is the sprawling SEA RANCH development with its miles of spectacular walking trails that hug the rugged coastline.

Water lovers may enjoy a canoe for two on the lazy Gualala River (from local commercial outfitters) or on Big River in MENDOCINO (from Stanford Inn by the Sea).

Farther north and inland, near GARBERVILLE, leave Highway 101 for a scenic, thirty-three-mile detour through the old redwoods along the Avenue of the Giants.

TABLES FOR TWO

The Olema Inn and Manka's in INVERNESS are good choices for travelers staying in the Point Reyes area. In OCCIDENTAL, the venerable Union Hotel serves popular Italian dishes on red-and-white checkered tablecloths.

St. Orres, the beautiful Russian-style inn located in GUALALA, has a well-respected dining room that serves fixed-price dinners. We've also enjoyed Ocean-song and Pangaea, both in Gualala.

If you find yourself in the vicinity of GARBERVILLE around dinner, try the Benbow Inn's romantically enchanting dining room, which is open to the public. In EUREKA, we and many visiting celebrities enjoy consistently memorable meals and fine wine in the dining room at Hotel Carter.

In MENDOCINO, we recommend Moosse Cafe on Kasten Street, Cafe BEAUJOLAIS, on Ukiah Street, and 955 Ukiah. These are within walking distance of our Mendocino destinations.

THE NORTH COAST

THE INN AT OCCIDENTAL

3657 Church Street
(P.O. Box 857)
Occidental, CA 95465
Telephone: (707) 874-1047;
toll-free: (800) 522-6324
Web site: www.innatoccidental.com

THE FACTS

Sixteen rooms and one cottage, each with private bath and fireplace. Most have spa tubs for two. Complimentary full breakfast served at communal dining-room table. Complimentary refreshments served every afternoon. Disabled access. Two-night minimum stay during weekends.

GETTING THERE

From Highway 101 north of Petaluma, take the Rohnert Park/Sebastopol/Highway 116 exit and follow west for seven and a half miles to Sebastopol. Turn left at the stoplight and follow toward Bodega Bay for six and a half miles. Turn right at the sign to Freestone and Occidental, and follow the Bohemian Highway for three and a half miles to the stop sign in Occidental. Turn right onto Church Street and follow uphill to inn.

We noticed the twinkling lights of this enchanting inn quite by accident during an after-dinner stroll around tiny Occidental. We were immediately impressed.

Nestled under tall trees on a gentle hillside, the inn is a three-level, century-old Victorian with an eclectic façade that includes brick, balconies, and gingerbread. It served as a private home for many generations and later became the site of the Occidental Water Bottling Company. The building was restored and refitted as an inn in the late 1980s.

ROOMS FOR ROMANCE

One of our favorite rooms is the Cut Glass Suite (low to mid $300 range), a private hideaway with its own garden, patio, and outdoor hot tub. Inside you'll find a king-sized art deco–style bed and collections of antique glass and contemporary photographs.

You'll have a view of the village church from the balcony of the Tiffany Suite (high $200 range), which also boasts a queen-sized, canopied, four-poster mahogany bed and an antique wood-burning fireplace. There's also a romantic shower for two. It's no surprise that this is a favorite honeymoon hideaway.

The Wine Country Room (around $300) celebrates viticulture with its cabernet-colored walls, an antique corkscrew collection, and a Prohibition-era still. This hideaway also has a cozy tub for two and a king-sized bed.

The whimsically styled Kitchen Cupboard Room (around $300) combines touches such as a vegetable-print Hermès scarf, a shadow-box collection of bone-handled carving sets, and an assortment of kitchen accessories.

Another favorite is the Marbles Suite (low $300 range), a corner room with a separate sitting area that's furnished with easy chairs and a couch and is warmed by a fireplace. There's also a spa tub for two set in its own romantic nook.

All the inn's rooms have private bathrooms with showers. Rates start in the mid $100 range.

POINT REYES SEASHORE LODGE

10021 Coastal Highway 1
(P.O. Box 39)
Olema, CA 94950
Telephone: (415) 663-9000;
toll-free: (800) 404-5634
Web site: www.pointreyesseashore.com

THE FACTS
Twenty-one rooms and cottages, each with private bath, wet bar/refrigerator, feather bed, and whirlpool tub. Complimentary continental breakfast. Conference facilities. Disabled access. Two-night minimum stay during weekends and holidays. Moderate to expensive.

GETTING THERE
The inn is two miles south of the community of Point Reyes Station on Highway 1. It's a one-hour drive from San Francisco and a two-and-a-half-hour drive from Sacramento.

While researching the first edition of *Weekends for Two* several years ago, we wanted to find an alternative to the quaint, antique inns that dot the Marin County coast. We didn't have to look far for this romanitic discovery, situated just off Highway 1 in tiny Olema.

Although it was built a century after many of the area's historic inns, Point Reyes Seashore Lodge was fashioned in a grand, graceful style that nonetheless fits right in with its Victorian neighbors. It's a great place from which to explore the bountiful beauty of this region.

The locale is a choice one: a hillside spot that commands a view of a meadow and a pine forest. Hidden by the building when you approach, the panorama is especially entrancing as it unfolds for the first time when you enter your room.

Guest rooms are compact, but the generous use of glass makes them appear much larger. Rooms along the upper floor have either bay windows or porches; some of the lower-level rooms have decks.

By the way, before setting off for weather-fickle Olema, be sure to bring clothing for both sun and fog, regardless of season. That is, unless you don't plan to leave your room. In that case, only the bare essentials are required.

ROOMS FOR ROMANCE

It is impossible to go wrong with any of the nine top-floor rooms. Some, however, are particularly well-suited to romance.

The Sir Francis Drake Suite (mid $200 range) is a split-level affair with a step-down, wood-paneled living space equipped with fireplace and refrigerator. A spectacular clerestory bay window rises from floor to ceiling, providing a view even from the four-poster feather bed in the elegant sleeping loft. Placement of the spa tub allows the bather an unusual opportunity to look out under the stairs through the window to the treetops beyond. There's room for two in the tub in a pinch.

Next door, the Garcia Rancho Suite (low $200 range) is a close second, with sleeping loft, spa tub, fireplace, and French doors that open onto a tiny deck. The Audubon Suite is similarly styled.

Terrace rooms with queen-sized beds, spa tubs for two, fireplaces, and flagstone patios are comparatively bargain priced in the mid to upper $100 range.

For convivial guests, continental breakfast can be taken in the downstairs dining room in front of a rock-walled fireplace. Those seeking more privacy may load their trays with pastries, juice, fruit, and cereal and retreat to their rooms.

THE FACTS

Four rooms, each with private bath and fireplace. Complimentary continental breakfast buffet at tables for two or more, or taken to your room. Spa. No disabled access. Two-night minimum stay during weekends; three-night minimum during holiday periods. Moderate to expensive.

GETTING THERE

The inn is located three blocks north of Point Reyes Station on Highway 1.

POINT REYES STATION INN

Most any weekend, when Tahoe- and beach-bound traffic has highways leading out of the Bay Area tied in knots, the smart money is cruising north. Driving through the lush pastures and hills of west Marin County, the two of you just might encounter more cows than cars.

You certainly won't encounter crowds at Point Reyes Station Inn, a small, upscale property set alongside Highway 1 about three blocks north of its tiny namesake community, once a stopping point for the old narrow-gauge railroad that rumbled up and down the coast. The newly constructed inn accommodates only four couples. Well-behaved canines are also welcome.

ROOMS FOR ROMANCE

Guest rooms here combine contemporary comforts with Old World elegance. For example, in the Victorian Room (around $200), an ornately carved antique bed and armoire are placed near a sumptuous contemporary spa tub for two.

Satinwood (around $200) is a romantic second-floor corner room with a cathedral ceiling and a small private balcony. Next door, the Eastlake Room is similarly styled.

POINT REYES STATION INN
11591 Highway 1
(P.O. Box 824)
Point Reyes Station, CA 94956
Telephone: (415) 663-9372
Web site: www.pointreyesstationinn.com

THE FACTS
*Sixteen rooms, each with private bath, spa tub for two,
gas fireplace, television, deck, and refrigerator. No in-room
phones. Restaurant. Disabled access. Smoking is allowed;
nonsmoking rooms available. Two-night minimum stay
during holiday periods. Moderate to expensive.*

GETTING THERE
*From the Bay Area, take Highway 101 past Santa Rosa to
River Road. Turn west onto Highway 116 and drive west
to Jenner. Head north on Highway 1 to Gualala. Driving
time from San Francisco is two and a half hours.*

Even with music playing softly, we could hear the not-so-distant nighttime surf pounding the Gualala beach. Add a flickering fire and you've got the fixings for a sensual feast that's well worth the two-and-a-half-hour drive from the Bay Area.

The inn's sixteen rooms are laid out in four clusters perched on a steep bluff overlooking the Pacific Ocean and the Gualala River. The river separates the inn from the beach, so the seashore, although very close, isn't immediately accessible on foot.

ROOMS FOR ROMANCE

Seacliff's rooms are compact but generously equipped. Each has a king-sized bed facing a fireplace and a small private deck. In the bathroom, a spa tub for two sits beneath an ocean-view window. The in-room refrigerator holds a complimentary bottle of champagne or sparkling cider. Bubblebath provides the perfect inspiration for a soak, assuming the two of you require any stimulus.

Although all rooms feature whitewater views and similar amenities, we suggest the upper-level accommodations for a bit more privacy and a slightly elevated river and ocean vista. The second-floor rooms also feature cathedral ceilings. All are offered in the mid to upper $100 range.

Seacliff staff are happy to transport guests who fly into Gualala's Ocean Ridge airport

SEACLIFF
39140 South Highway 1
(P.O. Box 1317)
Gualala, CA 95445
Telephone: (707) 884-1213
Web site: www.seacliffmotel.com

THE FACTS

Twenty-four oceanfront rooms, each with private bath, spa tub for two, deck, wet bar, refrigerator, and wood-burning fireplace. Complimentary continental breakfast is served in the lobby or may be taken to your room. Restaurant. Disabled access. Smoking is allowed in two rooms. Saturday stays and holiday periods require a two-night minimum. Moderate to expensive.

GETTING THERE

From Highway 101 at Santa Rosa, take the Guerneville/ River Road exit and follow River Road west to Guerneville. Take Highway 116 to Jenner, then drive north on Highway 1 to Gualala. The inn is on the left at the southern end of town, opposite the Gualala Hotel.

BREAKERS INN

39300 South Highway 1
(P.O. Box 389)
Gualala, CA 95445
Telephone: (707) 884-3200;
toll-free: (800) 273-2537
Web site: www.breakersinn.com

BREAKERS INN

One of the newer luxury hideaways on the Mendocino coast, Breakers Inn entices traveling couples with some of the most breathtaking ocean views available along the North Coast. However, views aren't the only attraction here. Breakers Inn also treats its guests to decadent amenities like fireplaces, comfortable decks, and large whirlpool tubs for two.

The four multitiered, dark wood-sided buildings that comprise the inn hug an ocean-view bluff at the mouth of the Gualala River. Gualala shops and restaurants are within a short walk of the inn. Those who are unwilling to tear themselves away from the inn for supper may dine at the Breakers' on-site ocean-view restaurant.

ROOMS FOR ROMANCE

The four rooms listed under the "luxurious spa room" category (mid $200 range) are the best in the house. In the stunning Japan room, for example, the centerpiece is an awesome handcrafted Japanese cypress spa tub for two. This fabulous room also has a four-poster rosewood bed and a sofa. Some of the luxury accommodations are also equipped with dry saunas.

You can't go wrong with the inn's "deluxe corner ocean-view rooms" (around $200) either. These spacious hideaways have corner fireplaces as well as sitting areas and beds set in alcoves with beveled glass windows. The San Francisco room offers what is arguably the Inn's best view, and it's furnished with a sleigh bed and leather furniture.

The largest upper-level room is Cape Cod, which has vaulted ceilings and offers sunset views. The Germany room has a king-sized, carved sleigh bed and a windowed corner sitting area with a sofa.

"Standard ocean-view rooms" are offered in the mid $100 range. Among these is Sweden, a sunny bluff-level room with a sleigh bed, and Connecticut, an upper-level room furnished in Shaker style with a four-poster bed.

Be aware that smoking is allowed in two rooms and that three "garden view rooms" have limited ocean views and standard private baths.

WHALE WATCH INN

35100 Highway 1
Gualala, CA 95445
Telephone: (707) 884-3667;
toll-free: (800) 942-5342
Web site: www.whalewatchinn.com

THE FACTS

Eighteen rooms and suites, each with private bath, fireplace, deck, bubble bath, and icemaker; several with spa tubs for two. No televisions or telephones in guest rooms. Complimentary full breakfast delivered to your room. Two-night minimum stay on weekends; three-night minimum on holiday weekends. Smoking permitted on decks only. Disabled access. Expensive to deluxe.

GETTING THERE

From the Bay Area, take Highway 101 past Santa Rosa to River Road. Go west on Highway 116 to Jenner. Head north on Highway 1 past Gualala. The inn is five miles north of Gualala at Anchor Bay on the west side of Highway 1. Driving time from San Francisco is two and a half hours.

WHALE WATCH INN

Unlike many North Coast inns, in which doilies and antiques prevail, the Whale Watch Inn dares to be different. With its pastel hues, interesting angles, and skylights, the inn offers a fresh touch of contemporary elegance and some of this region's most intimate rooms and soul-stirring views.

Occupying an unusual, sunny, banana-belt spot of the coast, Whale Watch Inn is spread among five separate buildings on two wooded acres. A private stairway leads to a half-mile-long beach with tidal pools and sea lions. It's the stuff of which honeymoons are made. You needn't worry that the bridal suite will be taken: each of Whale Watch Inn's eighteen rooms is honeymoon quality.

ROOMS FOR ROMANCE

We took special note of the fact that the "basics" at Whale Watch Inn are expensive amenities at many other destinations. The rooms all have an ocean view, a fireplace, and a private deck. But that's where the similarities end. Each accommodation has its own design, flow, and atmosphere.

The Bath Suite (high $200 range) is aptly named. While the sitting/sleeping area is impressive, wait until you ascend the spiral staircase. The Pacific-view spa tub for two set under a skylight makes this suite one of the inn's most popular. If you're planning a weekend visit, you'd be wise to make your reservation six months in advance.

Our home for a memorable stay was Crystal Sea (upper $200 range), which offers a coastal view that, in our opinion, is unsurpassed in Northern California. While the view through the wall of windows alone would have sufficed, we were also treated to an ocean-view deck as well as a moon and-stars view, thanks to a skylight over our bed. The room also boasts a raised fireplace and a two-person whirlpool bath.

Silver Mist (high $200 range), a split-level suite done in soft silver-gray and lavender, has an elevated dual spa tub that overlooks the fireplace and bed. Heartsong and Lovesong (mid $200 range) have deck-mounted hot tubs.

While some of our favorite rooms carry nightly rates at or near the $300 range (two-night minimum on weekends), Whale Watch Inn does offer accommodations that go a bit easier on the budget. At the time of our last visit, the Cygnet, Cliffside, and Morning Light rooms were offered at around $200 or less. All have fireplaces and nice ocean views; Morning Light has its own redwood dry sauna.

THE FACTS

*Six rooms in main house and four cottage rooms, each
with private bath, fireplace, and CD player. Tariff includes
breakfast and dinner for two. No disabled access. Two-night
minimum stay during weekends; three-night minimum
during holiday periods. Deluxe.*

GETTING THERE

*From the Bay Area, take Highway 101 to Cloverdale, then
drive west on Highway 128 for fifty-two miles to Highway 1.
Drive south on Highway 1 five miles to inn. Elk is approximately three hours by car from San Francisco.*

HARBOR HOUSE

5600 South Highway 1
(P.O. Box 369)
Elk, CA 95432
Telephone toll-free: (800) 720-7474
Web site: www.theharborhouseinn.com

"Impressive" is what the Goodyear Redwood Lumber Company had in mind when it built this 1916 house, an executive residence and exclusive retreat for VIP guests, as a stunning example of the beauty of redwood. Although its architectural style might best be described as craftsman or bungalow, a simple bungalow it isn't.

Wandering through the front door we found ourselves in a magnificent parlor lounge crafted entirely of redwood, with vaulted ceiling, hand-rubbed (with beeswax) paneling, and imposing fireplace. The entire inn is made of redwood, fashioned after an exhibit at the Panama-Pacific International Exposition in San Francisco.

The inn's ocean-view dining room is the primary center of activity, as the room rate includes not only breakfast but dinner for the two of you. Don't worry about having to make small talk with strangers, either. The proprietors of Harbor House have thoughtfully set the room with tables for two.

ROOMS FOR ROMANCE

After experiencing a parlor as grand as the one that greets visitors here, our expectations were on the high side as we toured the guest rooms. While not quite as awe-inspiring as the parlor, rooms are spacious and comfortable, and the ocean views rate four stars.

Rooms situated in the main house of many inns leave guests feeling as though they're swimming in a goldfish bowl, but the six rooms under the Harbor House roof are quiet and private.

Among our favorite accommodations is Harbor (mid $400 range including dinner), situated in a sunny corner on the second floor. A large room, it holds a king-sized Italian Renaissance bed and antique furniture that includes an English library table. This room also features a love seat set before a fireplace, an old-style bathroom with a shower, and a dramatic ocean view.

Beneath Harbor on the first floor is Cypress (mid $400 range including dinner), arguably the inn's most luxurious room, where the fireplace is flanked by windows with inspiring ocean and rock views. The bathroom has a clawfoot tub-and-shower combination. This room has its own ocean-view deck.

The Redwood and Greenwood rooms (low $300 range including dinner) face the front parking area and Highway 1.

Four quaint, red-and-white cottage rooms, each with a fireplace, complete the Harbor House estate. Our favorites are Seaview and Oceansong (low $400 range including dinner), both nicely redecorated since our last visit and both offering sweeping ocean views.

After you've savored the sea from a cottage deck or a guest-room window, head for the inn's gardens and the winding path that leads down to the water's edge. Along the way are sitting areas for sunning and relaxing.

THE FACTS

Fifteen rooms and cottages, each with private bath; most with fireplaces or woodstoves. Complimentary full buffet breakfast taken at tables for two. Complimentary afternoon refreshments. Full bar. Day spa. Saturday night stays require a two-night minimum; three-night minimum during holiday periods. Expensive to deluxe.

GETTING THERE

From the Bay Area, take Highway 101 to Cloverdale, then drive west on Highway 128 for fifty-two miles to Highway 1. At the end of Highway 128, turn left on Navarro River Bridge and drive south on Highway 1 for just over six miles to inn on right.

ELK COVE INN AND SPA

Whether your taste tilts to the crisp and contemporary or a simpler, more homespun environment, Elk Cove Inn has a hideaway with your names on it. The most eclectic of our North Coast destinations, the inn offers an intriguing mix of accommodations that take full advantage of the rugged coastal promontory on which the property is perched.

Like nearby Harbor House, the Elk Cove Inn has its roots in the lumber industry. Built in the late 1800s as a retreat for lumber company executives, the Victorian-style main house now shares the property with newer additions, including a group of cliff-hugging cottages.

A familiar landmark to North Coast travelers, this is one of the region's first bed-and-breakfast inns. Over the years it has seen a number of changes, most recently the addition of a day spa. Elk Cove Inn also has a delightful dining room and a full bar that serves some dangerously tasty martinis.

ROOMS FOR ROMANCE

In the inn's main house, we recommend Seascape (mid $200 range), a second-floor corner hideaway set under the eaves. The mustard-colored walls form intriguing angles; a corner fireplace and two flanking, ocean-view windows warm a cozy sitting area. The room has a king-sized bed and a shower for two. Next door, Baywatch (mid $200 range) also offers a great ocean view and a spa for two.

Our favorite Elk Cove Inn accommodations are the four "luxury spa suites" (low to mid $300 range) found in an adjacent newer, shingled building that also faces the sea. The two second-story units, the L. E. White room and the Sam McCanse room, have beamed ceilings, king-sized beds, and ocean-view balconies. All have gas fireplaces, craftsman-style furnishings, and spa tubs that are designed for one.

While many rooms at Elk Cove Inn boast very contemporary decor, some cottages and rooms have a decidedly seventies or even sixties feel. For example, the Surfsong Cottage (high $200 range), with its whimsical Arabian Knights theme, took us back a few decades, conjuring up memories of the San Francisco hippie era.

ELK COVE INN AND SPA
6300 South Highway 1
Elk, CA 95432
Telephone: (707) 877-3321
Web site: www.elkcoveinn.com

ALBION RIVER INN

3790 North Highway 1
(P.O. Box 100)
Albion, CA 95410
Telephone: (707) 937-1919;
toll-free: (800) 479-7944
Web site: www.albionriverinn.com

THE FACTS

Twenty-two rooms, each with private bath and fireplace; fourteen with oversized or spa tubs; twenty with private decks. Complimentary full breakfast served in dining room at tables for two. Restaurant and bar. Cooking classes and wine-maker dinners offered seasonally. Two-night minimum stay during weekends; three-night minimum stay during some holiday periods. Smoking is not permitted. Disabled access. Moderate to deluxe.

GETTING THERE

Albion is six miles south of Mendocino. From San Francisco, take Highway 101 north past Cloverdale. Head west on Highway 128 for fifty-two miles to Highway 1. Drive north two miles to inn on left. Driving time from San Francisco is approximately three and a half hours.

Who says cottages by the sea have to be old and rustic? Since we've found that most fit that description, we were surprised to discover Albion River Inn, a contemporary cluster of cozy, freestanding cottages (mixed with attractive multiroom units) designed specifically with today's selective romantic travelers in mind.

The inn's architecture is East Coast–inspired, but its setting is pure California coast. The Albion River empties into the ocean here, and each of the inn's twenty-two rooms affords views of this picturesque confluence of river and sea. Forested hills to the east provide the backdrop.

Rooms here go from the high $100 range for accommodations with a queen-sized bed, a shower, a fireplace, and an ocean-view deck, to the mid $300 range for a room with a spa tub, an ocean view, a deck, a fireplace, twin vanities, and a king-sized bed. The inn also operates a respected ocean-view restaurant that we found to be a delightful alternative to Mendocino eateries.

ROOMS FOR ROMANCE

Room 1 has a pitched roof and is equipped with a tiled fireplace that separates the king-sized bed from the bathroom. Room 5, a freestanding cottage, is similarly styled. Both have small private decks and spa tubs for two.

Room 20 is a particularly romantic hideaway with a king-sized bed placed before a tiled fireplace and a sitting area, as well as a spa tub set against an expansive ocean-view window.

Rates start in the mid $200 range for a very romantic room with an ocean view, a large soaking tub, and a fireplace and reach the mid $300 range for a sumptuously furnished room with a large spa tub and a fireplace.

We sampled Room 12 (mid $200 range), a wonderful hideaway offering a dynamite water view with a mesmerizing sound track courtesy of the pounding surf against the rocks below. We were able to savor the scene both from the room and from a pair of Adirondack chairs on the wooden deck. A fresh country theme is complemented by easy chairs set between a fireplace and a queen-sized bed. The bathroom contains a large soaking tub and a separate shower.

29

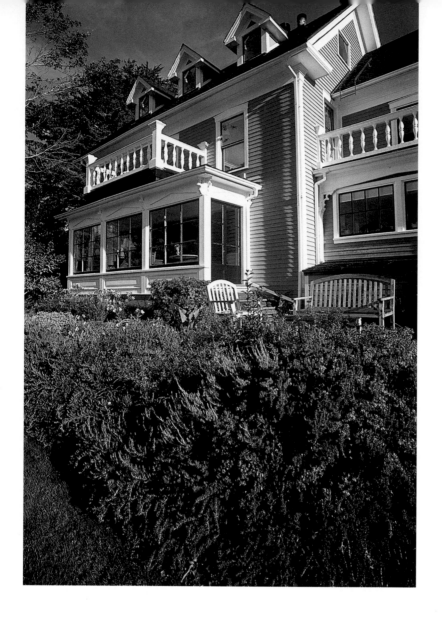

THE FACTS

Ten rooms, each with private bath; most with fireplaces and ocean views. Complimentary breakfast delivered to your room. Complimentary evening refreshments. No disabled access. Saturday stays require a two-night minimum; three-night minimum during holiday periods. Moderate to expensive.

GETTING THERE

From San Francisco, take Highway 101 north past Cloverdale. Drive west on Highway 128 for fifty-two miles to Highway 1. Turn north. The inn is a half-mile north of Little River and two miles south of Mendocino on Highway 1.

GLENDEVEN
8205 North Highway 1
Little River, CA 95456
Telephone: (707) 937-0083;
toll-free: (800) 822-4536
Web site: www.glendeven.com

GLENDEVEN

We pulled into the quiet burg of Little River on one of those sunny spring afternoons that make you want to call the office and quit your job. After checking into your room at Glendeven, you might even be tempted to sell the house and move north. Perhaps to protect guests from such crazy impulses, there are no phones at Glendeven.

From the road, passersby might mistake Glendeven for just another typically quaint bed-and-breakfast. Venture up the drive, however, and you'll be pleasantly surprised at the spaciousness and diversity of accommodations. As a couple of travelers well seasoned in sleuthing out places of the heart, we found Glendeven to be unsurpassed in romantic appeal.

ROOMS FOR ROMANCE

The handsome farmhouse, the centerpiece of the property, houses five guest rooms and a relaxing parlor. The Garret, a charming attic room with dormer windows (mid $100 range), faces the bay. The Eastlin Suite (low $200 range), also under the roof of the main house, offers a sitting room, a fireplace, a bay view through French doors, a private porch, and a king-sized rosewood bed. We sampled the first-floor Garden Room (mid $100 range), located just off the reception area. We found this room charming, but somewhat lacking in privacy.

A favorite hideaway for romantic getaways is Stevenscroft, a remote, four-room annex situated at the rear of the property. Upstairs, the high-ceilinged Briar Rose room (mid $200 range) overlooks the gardens and is decorated in French country style.

We were also lucky enough to spend a memorable afternoon and night in Pinewood (low $200 range), situated on the lower level of Stevenscroft. Redecorated in recent years along with Glendeven's other rooms, the Pinewood room is paneled in its namesake wood and features a cozy nook affording a sweeping view to the distant bay. Wood arranged neatly in the fireplace awaited only a match. French doors open onto a private ocean- and garden-view deck.

On our first afternoon here, a walk through the woods to the ocean headlands was among our well-intentioned diversion options. But the room's romantic magic kept us indoors.

Apparently, we weren't the only couple to be lulled by Glendeven's sensual charms, as a detailed room diary described the rendezvous of scores of previous Pinewood guests. Skimming through the entries we paused at one particularly intriguing account of a visit by Chuck and Patty. Several pages (and only a couple of months) later, we found another Chuck and Patty entry—with even greater raves. Maybe Glendeven is even better the second or third time around.

THE FACTS

Seven rooms, each with private bath. Six rooms have fire-
places. Complimentary full breakfast delivered to your room.
Complimentary afternoon tea and cookies. Two-night mini-
mum stay during weekends; three- or four-night minimum
stay during holidays. Disabled access. Moderate to expensive.

GETTING THERE

From Highway 101, drive west on Highway 128 for fifty-two
miles to Highway 1. Drive north on Highway 1. In Mendocino,
turn left at the traffic light onto Little Lake Road and drive
two blocks to Howard Street. Turn left and follow to inn
on right.

HEADLANDS INN
Corner of Howard and Albion Streets
(P.O. Box 132)
Mendocino, CA 95460
Telephone: (707) 937-4431;
toll-free: (800) 354-4431
Web site: www.headlandsinn.com

HEADLANDS INN

MENDOCINO

Don't let the Headlands Inn's "downtown" location scare you away. With not a single stoplight except on the highway and a main street that's only about four blocks long, Mendocino isn't exactly fraught with noise and congestion—unless, of course, you count the crashing surf and circling seagulls.

This distinctive Mendocino charmer began life as John Barry's barbershop in 1868, and it has since served stints as a restaurant, a hotel annex, and, more recently, a private residence. These days, its cozy rooms are home to traveling romantics who enjoy a comfy, informal, bed-and-breakfast experience.

ROOMS FOR ROMANCE

The largest room in the house and one of our favorites is the Bessie Strauss (low $200 range) on the second floor. This sunny corner room has a wood-burning fireplace, a king-sized feather bed, a love seat, and a table and chairs set in a bay window that looks over the garden to the ocean.

Guests in the third-floor John Barry Room (mid $100 range) can relax under a gabled ceiling or curl up on the dormer-window love seat and enjoy the fireplace. Under the eaves, wallpapered in soft colors, sits a queen-sized feather bed. This room commands a spectacular ocean view.

Guests staying in the W. J. Wilson Room (mid $100 range) are treated to a gorgeous bay view, a wood-burning stove, and a queen-sized, four-poster feather bed. The private deck is set adjacent to a classic Mendocino water tower.

On the third floor, the George Switzer Room (mid $100 range) has a handsome fireplace and cozy garret window seats from which to savor a distant ocean view.

For privacy seekers, the homespun Casper Cottage (high $100 range) is detached from the main house and comes complete with a television and a small refrigerator, perfect for chilling a bottle of bubbly. The cottage is furnished with a queen-sized, four-poster bed and a large bathroom with an extra-long tub for two.

33

THE FACTS

Ten rooms, each with private bath; six with fireplaces. Complimentary full breakfast served at a communal table or outside, weather permitting. Limited disabled access. Two-night minimum stay during weekends and summer months; three- to- four-night minimum during holidays. Moderate to expensive.

GETTING THERE

From the Bay Area, follow Highway 101 past Cloverdale; west on Highway 128 for fifty-two miles, and north on Highway 1. In Mendocino, turn left at Little Lake Road (at stoplight); inn is on the right. Driving time from San Francisco via Highway 101 is approximately three and a half hours; driving all the way on twisting Highway 1 takes about five hours.

JOSHUA GRINDLE INN
44800 Little Lake Road
(P.O. Box 647)
Mendocino, CA 95460
Telephone: (707) 937-4143
Web site: www.joshgrin.com

JOSHUA GRINDLE INN

In this quaint community, where bed-and-breakfast spots are as plentiful as seagulls, the Joshua Grindle Inn is a standout. Framed on a pretty knoll by a white picket fence and the bluest of California skies (when the fog's not around, that is), Mr. Grindle's old Victorian homestead is quintessential Mendocino.

Since our last visit, new innkeepers Charles and Cindy Reinhart have introduced many upgrades and renovations, ensuring the inn's place among the most romantic on the North Coast.

ROOMS FOR ROMANCE

Half of the ten rooms (each has a private bath) are located in the main house, built over a hundred years ago by the inn's namesake, town banker Joshua Grindle. The Grindle (low $200 range), Joshua's bedroom, offers both ocean and bay views, and a cozy, sleigh-style couch set under the eaves.

The handsome Master room (mid $200 range) has a wood-manteled fireplace and a recently remodeled luxury bathroom with a spa tub for two, a separate shower, and a view of the garden and trees.

The Saltbox Cottages and Watertower buildings set privately at the rear of the grounds are our personal favorites. Watertower I (around $200), our room for a night, occupies most of the ground floor of the tower, a replica (complete with inward-sloping walls) of the many vintage water towers that dot the community. The spacious room is furnished in comfortable country style with pine furnishings. A small wood-burning stove sits on a corner brick hearth with wood stacked neatly in a tiny antique wheelbarrow. The bathroom has a deep soaking tub and a shower.

Watertower II on the second floor is similarly furnished and, although a bit smaller than the room below, offers a nicer city view with a peek of the ocean through windows on three sides.

In the Saltbox Cottage, South Cypress (mid $200 range) is a private and spacious retreat with an open-beam ceiling. The room has a queen-sized bed and a fireplace, and the bathroom holds a whirlpool tub for one and a separate shower. Next door, the slightly more masculine North Cypress boasts similar niceties. These two rooms are equipped with televisions, videocassette/DVD players, and CD players.

THE FACTS

Thirty-three rooms and suites, each with private bath, fireplace, and CD, videocassette, and DVD players. Complimentary full breakfast served at tables for two in dining room. Vegetarian restaurant. Swimming pool and spa. Bicycle, canoe, and kayak rentals. Massage services and yoga classes. Disabled access. Pets welcome. Saturday stays generally require a two-night minimum; three-night minimum during holidays. Expensive to deluxe.

GETTING THERE

From San Francisco, take Highway 101 north past Cloverdale. Drive west on Highway 128 to Highway 1 and go north. The inn is just off Highway 1 at the mouth of Big River on the southern outskirts of Mendocino.

STANFORD INN BY THE SEA
Highway 1 and Comptche-Ukiah Road
(P.O. Box 487)
Mendocino, CA 95460
Telephone: (707) 937-5615;
toll-free: (800) 331-8884
Web site: www.stanfordinn.com

A quick stroll around the grounds might lead you—at least initially—to conclude that Stanford Inn by the Sea is a perfect getaway destination for active couples. However, open the door to your room and even the most athletic-minded couples might decide to simply kick back and relax.

If you enjoy the out-of-doors, there are acres of landscaped and wild grounds to explore, gardens to tour, and even llamas and horses to pet. There's a greenhouse-enclosed swimming pool, spa, and sauna, and the inn loans mountain bikes to guests and rents kayaks and canoes for exploring Big River, which is just a short walk from your room.

For those not motivated to wander, views of the grounds, llamas, and more can be had from the comfort of your own deck. And there are plenty of additional niceties—besides each other—to keep the two of you occupied.

No expense has been spared in creature comforts here. Rooms are paneled in tasteful pine and are furnished with king- or queen-sized, four-poster feather beds, down comforters, and upscale linens. All have wood-burning fireplaces or wood stoves, refrigerators, and French doors, and are stocked with complimentary coffee, chocolate truffles, juice, and local wine. Each also has a remote-controlled television as well as a videocassette, DVD, and CD player. There are computers in the lobby for e-mail and for checking the Internet.

ROOMS FOR ROMANCE

While the decor varies slightly throughout the inn, you can't go wrong with any of the rooms. Some do have more dramatic views than others: for the best views of Mendocino village and the picturesque bay, ask whether rooms 7 through 12 on the lower floor or rooms 23 through 26 on the upper floor might be available. The decks on the upper floors offer more privacy.

Most oft requested are the Bishop Pine Suite, Bishop Pine Room, and Grand Fir. These large and private accommodations occupy the top floor of the Forest Building and have vaulted ceilings and grand views of the Mendocino Headlands.

Room rates start in the mid $200 range. One-bedroom suites range in price from the high $300 range to the mid $400 range. There are also two-bedroom suites and suites with kitchen facilities. The inn welcomes pets; there's an extra charge of around $25 for your animal companion.

The inn's newer spa in the Forest Building offers massage and yoga classes.

THE FACTS

Ten rooms, each with private bath. Complimentary full breakfast served at a large communal table and smaller tables or delivered to your room. No disabled access. Saturday night stays require two-night minimum. Moderate to expensive.

GETTING THERE

Fort Bragg is about ten miles north of Mendocino. Highway 1 becomes Main Street in Fort Bragg. From Main Street downtown, turn west on Pine Street and follow for one block. Turn right on Stewart Street. Inn is on the right.

THE WELLER HOUSE

524 Stewart Street
Fort Bragg, CA 95437
Telephone toll-free: (877) 8WELLER
Web site: www.wellerhouse.com

Mendocino may be the ultimate destination of most northbound getaway travelers on Highway 1, but we continue to hear from readers interested in suitable accommodations in Fort Bragg, a more commercialized coastal community about ten minutes north.

Our most recent Fort Bragg discovery is the Weller House, which we happened upon not long after the property had emerged from a fairly significant renovation and restoration. Considered Fort Bragg's most historically significant building, the Weller House is the only structure in town that has earned a place on the National Register of Historic Places.

And what a place it is. A gingerbread-laced Victorian mansion built in 1886, the inn occupies a large, nicely landscaped lot one block from Fort Bragg's bustling Main Street at the edge of a quaint neighborhood. It's only a short walk to the aptly named Glass Beach, with its pebblelike sand. At the time of this revision, the famous Skunk Train, which has a station within walking distance of the inn, had reemerged from financial troubles and was again offering passenger service through the forested mountains.

ROOMS FOR ROMANCE

Former professional musicians, innkeepers Ted and Eva Kidwell (Eva was born and raised in Sweden) have upgraded the property since taking over in the late 1990s and have created a number of rooms suitable for a romantic getaway.

In the main house, we liked Tulip (mid $100 range), the inn's largest room. Features here include a stained-glass bay window and a bathroom equipped with a six-foot-long old-fashioned tub, definitely big enough for two.

Aqua (mid to upper $100 range), offers a large bathroom with a corner spa tub for two, a stained-glass window, and a peek at the distant ocean.

The two of you will be especially intrigued by the accommodations in the stately, renovated water tower that stands behind the mansion. There we discovered a pair of more contemporary-style rooms. On the ground level is Raven (upper $100 range), a cozy room with a king-sized bed, a spa tub, and an almost hidden shower tucked behind the tub. This room has an ocean view. On the level above is Heather, a smaller room offering more of an ocean view along with a queen-sized brass bed, three chairs, and a small bathroom with a shower.

Eva led us up the stairs to the next level, where we expected to find another guest chamber. Instead we discovered a large communal hot tub with an expansive view of the community and the ocean. Those unfazed by heights may venture up even farther, to the very top of the water tower—reportedly the highest point in Fort Bragg.

Back in the main house, a nine-hundred-square-foot ballroom occupies the inn's third level. This impressive space, which is paneled in original redwood, serves as a comfy parlor area and the inn's dining room. Windows here look out to sea.

THE FACTS

Fifty-five rooms, each with private bath. Complimentary English tea and scones served each afternoon. Restaurant serves breakfast, lunch, and dinner. Golf course, swimming, and boating nearby. Closed January through March. No disabled access. Certain time periods and special events require minimum night stays. Moderate to deluxe.

GETTING THERE

From San Francisco, follow Highway 101 north for approximately three and a half hours. Two miles south of Garberville, exit Highway 101 at Lake Benbow Drive. The inn is on the left, adjacent to the highway.

BENBOW INN

445 Lake Benbow Drive
Garberville, CA 95440
Telephone: (707) 923-2124;
toll-free: (800) 355-3301
Web site: www.benbowinn.com

BENBOW INN

After miles and miles of exacting albeit beautiful twists and turns along densely wooded Highway 101, the Benbow Inn emerges through the trees as the proverbial pot of gold.

Designed by Albert Farr, who created Jack London's famous Wolf House in Glen Ellen, the Benbow was built in an era when remote resort hotels were considered destinations where travelers nested for extended periods. The 1920s-era inn attracted guests who stayed for days—even weeks—enjoying golf, fishing, swimming, and boating. It offered vacationers, including Hollywood stars and other famous folks, all the trappings of a world-class resort, only on a smaller scale.

While other establishments of those days have gone to seed, the years—and owners—have been kinder to the Benbow Inn. The latest proprietors have continued to infuse life into the stately Tudor-style structure, making improvements while preserving its historic grace and charm.

During the warm summer months, a dam is erected on the Eel River adjacent to the property, creating an old-fashioned swimming lake.

ROOMS FOR ROMANCE

A reconnaissance stroll around the main hotel and the adjacent wings revealed many rooms worthy of a weekend getaway. A few stand out, nonetheless. For example, we spent the night in room 108 (around $200) on the lower level of the Terrace, a separate, two-story wing adjacent to the historic building. Our room and the others in this wing overlook a huge lawn encircled by tall trees. The river is just beyond the trees.

Our large, wallpapered room was decorated in rich red tones and featured lots of dark wood trim. Two wing chairs, a small desk, a large armoire, and a king-sized four-poster bed completed the picture. Outside was our own garden patio overlooking the lawn. Although Highway 101 runs by the property, we weren't bothered by traffic noise.

Upper Terrace units have decks with great river views. One of these, room 110, is a huge accommodation, with a fireplace, a king-sized bed, an expanse of windows, a love seat, and attractive antiques. The large outdoor deck holds a table and chairs and two lounge chairs.

In the charming historic building, nice rooms with king-sized beds are available from the mid $100 range.

The inn's enchanting dining room, still furnished with the original tables and chairs, is a delightful place to dine at the end of a lazy day.

THE FACTS

Twelve rooms, each with private bath, telephone, and CD player. Complimentary full breakfast served in dining room at tables for two. Televisions available. Restaurant. Two-night minimum stay during certain weekend and holiday periods. Moderate.

GETTING THERE

From Highway 101, fifteen miles south of Eureka, take Ferndale exit. Drive five miles west to Main Street. Inn is downtown on the corner of Ocean and Main.

THE VICTORIAN INN

400 Ocean Avenue
(P.O. Box 96)
Ferndale, CA 95536
Telephone: (707) 786-4949;
toll-free: (888) 589-1808
Web site: www.a-victorian-inn.com

THE VICTORIAN INN

Judging from the cameras aimed in the direction of this architectural masterpiece during our brief visit, The Victorian Inn is doing its part to keep the Kodak company in business. One of Northern California's most frequently photographed buildings, The Victorian Inn has been stopping traffic since its construction by a town banker back in 1890.

Resplendent in colorful Victoriana, the inn sits among other gingerbread-laden buildings in downtown Ferndale, a town seemingly forgotten by time. After all, there aren't too many California towns in which a "mercantile establishment" and a saddlery still thrive.

The downstairs portion of this grand, redwood-hewn building is devoted to a jewelry shop operated by the innkeepers, as well as an independently operated restaurant. Guest rooms are upstairs.

ROOMS FOR ROMANCE

Among the inn's dozen rooms, we found the suites and other more expensive accommodations to be the best suited to romantic getaways. Our recommendations include the Victorian Parlor (mid $100 range), which has a bay window seat overlooking Ferndale's Main Street. It has a king-sized bed, a floral carpet, and a bathroom with old-fashioned honeycomb tile floor.

The nicely appointed Ira Russ Suite (upper $100 range) is named after the inn's builder, and this room was his favorite. This corner suite boasts a king-sized brass bed and a curtained turret sitting area overlooking Main Street and Ocean Avenue. The large bathroom holds an old-fashioned tub with a brass shower fixture. Next door, the namesake room of Ira's sister Maggie has a romantic in-room bath chamber that's curtained off from the bedroom.

We also recommend the spacious Viola McBride Room with its Main Street views and black marble-tiled bathroom floor; and the Pacifica Room, a bright corner hideaway with a wood-burning fireplace and a turreted sitting area. Both of these rooms carry rates in the upper $100 range.

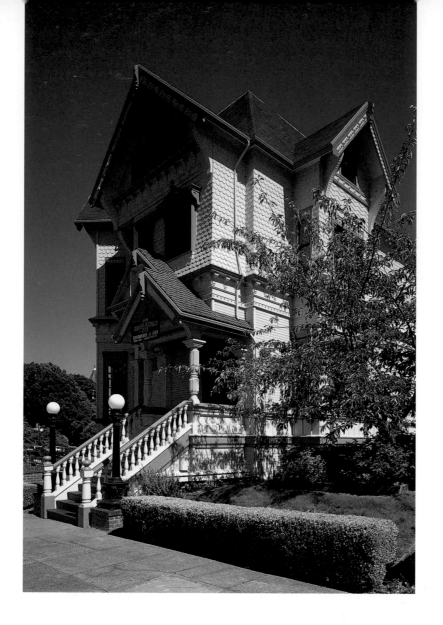

THE FACTS

Thirty-four rooms and suites, each with private bath, enter-tainment center, telephone, and television; many with fire-places and spa tubs for two. Complimentary full breakfast served in the restaurant or in your room. Complimentary late-afternoon and evening refreshments. Restaurant. Disabled access. No minimum stay required. Moderate to deluxe.

GETTING THERE

From Highway 101 in downtown Eureka, drive west on L Street through Old Town to the corner of Third and L Streets.

CARTER HOUSE INNS
301 L Street,
Eureka, CA 95501
Telephone: (707) 444-8062;
toll-free: (800) 404-1390
Web site: www.carterhouse.com

Little did Eureka native son Mark Carter know, a couple of decades ago, that a romantic small-town family adventure would blossom into not only a new life's work but a successful food, wine, and lodging enterprise that would become known throughout the country.

It was on a corner of Old Town Eureka that Mark, a true Renaissance man, set about building a grand manor house for his family, guided by plans originally drafted by Joseph Newsome, whose landmark Carson Mansion stands just a stone's throw away. Over a two-year period, Mark and a three-person crew built the imposing, four-story redwood manor themselves, following every Victorian detail in the architect's plan. However, Mark, his wife Christi, and their children soon felt overwhelmed by the size of the manse, and they decided to convert the still-new structure into a first-class country inn, The Original Carter House.

Next came the handsome Victorian-style Hotel Carter, built from scratch on the opposite corner. Since then, Mark has added a pair of restored Victorian cottages and opened the critically acclaimed Restaurant 301 in the hotel. He also began crafting fine namesake wines that are turning up on the wine lists of a growing number of restaurants. No surprise that the Carter collection has played host to such notables as Barbra Streisand, James Brolin, Steven Spielberg, and jazz chanteuse Diana Krall.

THE ORIGINAL CARTER HOUSE

While many Victorians are dark by design, Mark deviated from the traditional slightly to give the grand mansion a bright, airy look. This was accomplished by adding bay windows and painting interior walls in lighter shades. The extra light is especially appreciated during those sometimes foggy coastal days.

The Carters' former living area on the second floor has become the inn's showplace suite (low $400 range), featuring a fireplace, an extra bedroom, a spa tub for two, and a bright and cheery bathroom with tiled floor and oak trim. There's also a communal kitchen on the second floor where coffee is available.

On the third floor is the Burgundy Room (mid $300 range), actually a suite with a king-sized, canopied bed and a private bath with a tub-and-shower combination. The oft photographed Carson Mansion is visible from this suite. A harbor view is available from a gabled window in the Blue Room next door.

The six rooms here are decorated with Oriental rugs, fresh flowers, original art, and fluffy comforters, and flannel robes await the guests.

Continued on page 47

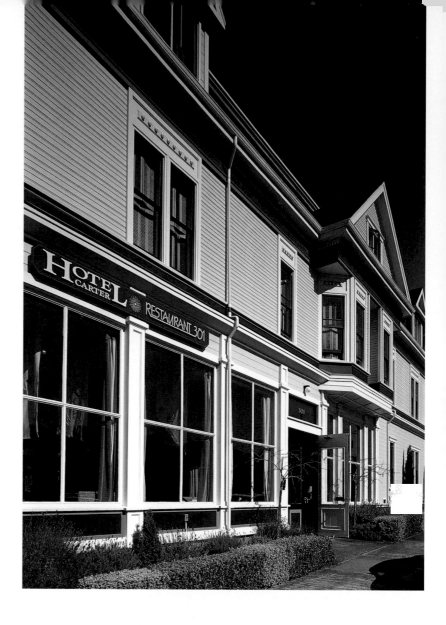

Continued from page 45

THE HOTEL CARTER

Modeled after a nineteenth-century Eureka hostelry, the hotel displays the same attention to detail as the mansion across the street. A selection of particularly romantic suites is found under the eaves on the hotel's third floor. These are furnished with queen-sized beds, original art, marble fireplaces, sitting areas, and entertainment centers with televisions, videocassette players, and CD players. They're also romantically equipped with oversized, double-head showers and whirlpool tubs for two.

Our suite for a night, room 302, holds a step-up, deep spa tub for two under a window with views of the marina, the Carson Mansion, and the nearby Victorian Pink Lady, another local architectural landmark. A sitting room with a tiled, wood-burning fireplace and a couch is separated from the sleeping chamber by French doors. The bathroom is equipped with an oversized shower with dual spigots. Deluxe rooms and suites in the hotel are priced in the mid $200 range to the low $300 range.

On the inn's first floor are several standard guest rooms along with a parlor, a registration area, and Mark's Restaurant 301, which boasts an extensive wine list that reads like veritable book. Mark also operates a wine club accessible through the Carter House Web site.

THE COTTAGES

On our most recent visit to Eureka, we spent a memorable night in the Carter Cottage (starting at around $500), a self-contained, honeymoon-quality hideaway that sits next door to the mansion. Decorated in a bright and playful mix of French and Southwest themes, the refurbished turn-of-the-century cottage has a large living area with comfortable chairs, a sofa, a gas fireplace, and a large dining table. The adjacent kitchen is equipped with commercial-quality appliances; the staff will fix dinner here for the two of you at an additional cost.

The ultra-romantic bedroom features another fireplace, a canopied and draped king-sized bed, and French doors that open to a wonderful tiled bathroom with one of the most inviting spa tubs we've experienced; it's custom designed for two. A huge outdoor deck offers a peek of Humboldt Bay and the colorful Carson Mansion down the street.

Next door, the ornate Bell Cottage (high $100 to mid $200 range) holds three impressive rooms as well as common parlor rooms and a kitchen. The rooms here, perfect for romantic getaways, are furnished with nice antiques and art from the Carters' personal collection. Bathrooms are ultra-contemporary and feature spa tubs for two.

DAYTIME DIVERSIONS

After you've visited a few of the more famous wineries in Napa and Sonoma Valleys, turn off onto some of the less traveled roads and visit a small winery or two. One of our favorites is **Chateau Montelena** on Tubbs Lane off Highway 29, outside of **CALISTOGA**. Walk around back for a look at the winery's medieval-style façade. While you're there, take a look at the spectacular oriental garden complete with lake, teahouses, and an old Chinese junk.

The Hess Collection, on Redwood Road in the Mayacamas Mountains above **NAPA,** blends the owner's fabulous international art collection with the art of making wine.

For a different perspective, try the **Napa Valley Wine Train** on its brunch or dinner runs along Highway 29. A number of companies offer early-morning **balloon flights** over the valley floor. Your hotel/inn staff can provide names of operators.

A less lofty but still stunning valley vista is served up, along with local wines, on the view deck at **Auberge du Soleil** (see listing).

The northern Napa Valley community of **CALISTOGA** is home to several spas and hot springs where you can enjoy a soothing **mud bath and massage.**

TABLES FOR TWO

For a memorable romantic meal, we recommend the candlelit, French-themed **Domaine Chandon** Restaurant in **YOUNTVILLE. Mustard's Grill** on Highway 29, also in Yountville, continues to rank as one of the valley's best restaurants for lunch or dinner.

In northern Napa Valley, personal favorites include Pat Kuleto's **Martini House** and **Tra Vigne,** both in **ST. HELENA.** In **CALISTOGA,** try **Catahoula, Brannan's Grill,** or **Wappo Bar.**

In **SONOMA,** we enjoy the Portuguese cuisine at Manuel Azevedo's **LaSalette** restaurant on Highway 12, as well as **The Girl and the Fig** and **Della Santina's,** both near Sonoma Square.

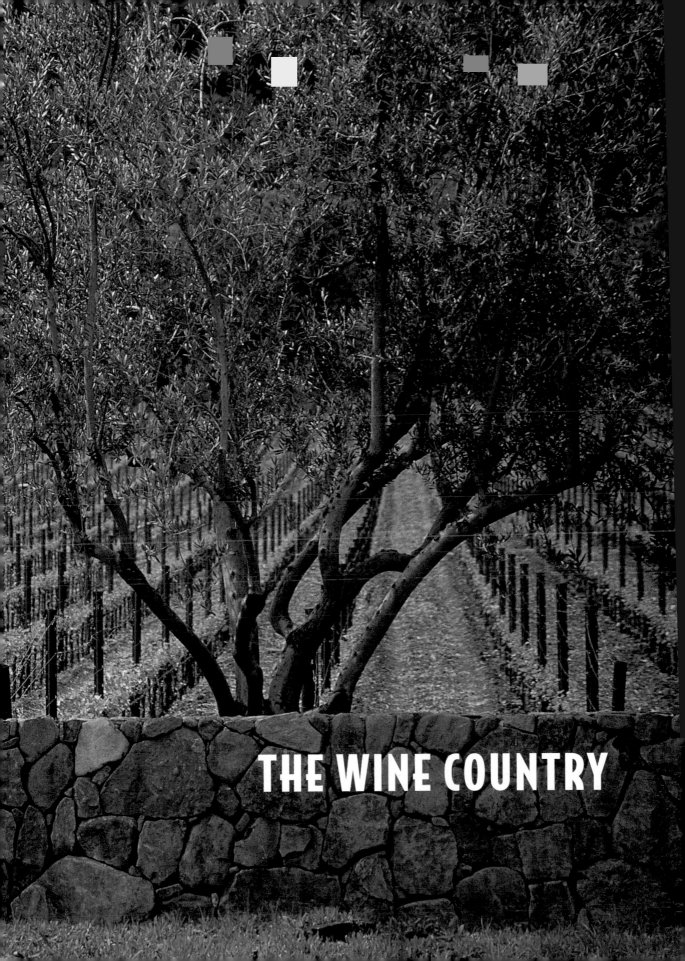

THE WINE COUNTRY

THE FACTS

Fifty-five rooms, each with private bath; many with wood-burning fireplaces. Complimentary champagne breakfast buffet optionally delivered to your room. Swimming pool and spa. Fitness center and sauna. Round-the-clock concierge service. Two-night minimum stay during weekends; three-night minimum during holiday periods. Deluxe.

GETTING THERE

From Highway 29 in Yountville, take the Madison Street exit. Hotel is on corner of Madison and Washington Streets.

NAPA VALLEY LODGE

While researching new destinations in Napa Valley, we rediscovered this not-so-new lodge as it emerged from a five-million-dollar makeover. Well-known at least by sight to veteran Highway 29 travelers, Yountville's first hotel sits adjacent to the highway, behind vineyards at the northern edge of town.

Outside, the lodge's two-decades-old façade has been given a handsome face-lift, boasting Tuscan-style architecture with clay-tiled roofs, arched loggias, and terra-cotta walkways. Behind the property and adjacent to a vineyard is an inviting swimming pool area, perfect for those warm Napa Valley summers.

The lodge is operated by the Woodside Hotels and Resorts chain, which caters to business conference clientele in addition to weekend romantics.

ROOMS FOR ROMANCE

The newly restyled guest rooms feature private balconies and terraces, large bathrooms, and cushy beds with duvets. For a romantic getaway, we recommend the rooms in the Deluxe Fireplace and Luxury Suite categories.

Deluxe Fireplace Rooms (mid $300 range) feature cozy sitting areas with couches in addition to fireplaces. Bathrooms are oversized and well equipped.

The suites (mid $400 range) measure nearly six hundred square feet and overlook the garden, pool, and adjacent vineyard. Suites boast comfortable living rooms, separate bedrooms with limestone fireplaces, and gorgeous bathrooms equipped with soaking tubs for two and separate showers.

We especially liked the comparatively remote and quieter wing housing rooms 23 through 25 on the ground floor and rooms 53 through 55 on the upper floor.

NAPA VALLEY LODGE
2230 Madison Street
Yountville, CA 94599
Telephone: (707) 944-2468;
toll-free: (800) 368-2468
Web site: www.napavalleylodge.com

THE FACTS

Fifty-two rooms and nineteen suites, each with private bath; most with fireplaces and tubs for two. Twenty-four-hour room service, videocassette movie library, swimming pool/spa (heated year-round and open round-the-clock), day spa, steam sauna, exercise room, beauty salon, tennis courts with staff pro, and massage service. Restaurant. Smoking is allowed. Disabled access. Two-night minimum stay during weekends; three-night minimum during holiday periods. Deluxe.

GETTING THERE

Take Highway 29 north past Napa. At Rutherford, drive east on Route 128, turn left on the Silverado Trail, and then make an immediate right on Rutherford Hill Road to resort.

AUBERGE DU SOLEIL
180 Rutherford Hill Road
Rutherford, CA 94573
Telephone: (707) 963-1211
Web site: www.aubergedusoleil.com

AUBERGE DU SOLEIL

After checking in at Auberge du Soleil one lovely winter afternoon, we hurried straight through our sumptuous room to the private deck. There we settled, savoring the day's final hours of warm sunshine along with the splendid valley scene beyond. Returning to the deck the next morning, we watched hot-air balloons float above a dreamy valley mist.

This exquisite, French-style, full-service inn, set on a wooded hillside just off the Silverado Trail, is one of few Wine Country inns that afford panoramic valley vistas. And Auberge du Soleil was built with the view in mind. The inn's rooms and suites are spread among eleven cottages over thirty-three acres. All have private, spacious decks overlooking Napa Valley and the hills beyond.

ROOMS FOR ROMANCE

The cottages, named after French provinces, are set above and below a long driveway. The lower units—Versailles, Provence, Normandie, Armagnac, Lorraine, Picardie, and Alsace—offer unobstructed valley views and the most privacy. Rooms are styled throughout in comfortable Mediterranean/Southwest decor and Mexican tiles. Covered patio decks are private enough for lounging in the white terry robes provided in each room. Rates during harvesttime start in the upper $400 range for a standard room with a king-sized bed. A room with a spa tub for two carries a tariff in the low $500 range. Suites command $700 or more.

Our room for a night, Versailles Eight, has a king-sized bed and overlooks the valley and the resort's championship tennis courts. We particularly enjoyed the fireplace's proximity to the bed. Versailles One, a one-bedroom suite, is another often requested room.

A subsequent visit brought us to Picardie, a spacious one-bedroom suite with a large living room. The living room fireplace was visible from our bed.

The bathrooms at Auberge du Soleil merit particular mention. Each has a large dual tub (spa tubs in deluxe rooms) illuminated by a skylight. Some even boast sexy, tiled showers with double showerheads.

THE FACTS
Twenty-one rooms, each with private bath and fireplace.
Complimentary continental breakfast served at tables for
two or in your room. Restaurant, swimming pool, and commu-
nal spa. Two-night minimum stay during weekends. Deluxe.

GETTING THERE
Take Highway 29 north past Napa and drive to St. Helena.
The inn is located next to Merryvale Winery on the east
side of Highway 29 on the southern edge of town. Highway
29 becomes Main Street in St. Helena.

THE INN AT SOUTHBRIDGE

The people who operate Meadowood Napa Valley resort (see listing) created this sleek sister establishment near the heart of St. Helena, just off Highway 29 and within a short walk of some of our favorite Wine Country shops and dining spots.

This contemporary-style property was conceived by William Turnbull Jr., who designed Sterling Vineyards, Cakebread Wine Cellars, and his own namesake winery. The inn features skylights, vaulted ceilings, and French doors. Many rooms overlook a central tree-covered courtyard. The warm colors reflect the vineyards and nearby hills.

For around $25 extra, couples staying here have privileges at Meadowood's tennis courts, spa, and fitness center. Meadowood is about two miles away in the hills. Guests also have privileges at a spa and fitness center adjacent to The Inn at Southbridge.

THE INN AT SOUTHBRIDGE

1020 Main Street
St. Helena, CA 94574
Telephone: (707) 967-9400
Web site: www.innatsouthbridge.com

ROOMS FOR ROMANCE

Accommodations here are anything but fussy, and the decor varies little from room to room. Guest-room walls are buttery yellow, and the minimalist wood furnishings have clean lines. Rooms open to small Juliet balconies. King-sized beds are covered with comforters, and two chairs sit before a wood-burning fireplace. Bathrooms have tub-and-shower combinations.

Nightly weekend rates start in the mid $400 range for a room with a king-sized bed. Suites cost about $600. Winter and weekday rates are somewhat less expensive.

THE FACTS

Fifty-four rooms, each with private bath; most with fireplaces. Two swimming pools/spas. Complimentary extended continental breakfast buffet in breakfast room at indoor and outdoor tables for two. Wine and beer bar. Spa services. Bicycle rentals. Smoking is allowed in some areas. Disabled access. Moderate to deluxe.

GETTING THERE

Take Highway 29 north past Napa to St. Helena. The inn is at the southern edge of town on Highway 29, which becomes Main Street in St. Helena.

HARVEST INN
1 Main Street
St. Helena, CA 94574
Telephone: (707) 963-9463;
toll-free: (800) 950-8466
Web site: www.harvestinn.com

HARVEST INN

Queen of Hearts, Count of Fantasy, Earl of Ecstasy . . . with names like these, it's clear the creators of Harvest Inn weren't designing rooms with sleeping foremost in mind. Not that you won't get a good night's sleep here. It's just that there are so many other, er, things to do.

One of the more innocent—although pleasant—pastimes at Harvest Inn is a stroll around the grounds. Clusters of Tudor-style buildings set on seven colorful, lush acres give the feeling of an Old World English village. The intricate brick and stonework of the walkways and chimneys earned mention in *Smithsonian* magazine. The use of brick is carried into the guest rooms, where expansive fireplaces are common.

ROOMS FOR ROMANCE

On a recent visit, we luxuriated in Knight of Knights, a sumptuous split-level suite located in the aristocratic, eight-room Manor House, where accommodations overlook a sweep of vineyards and the tree-carpeted mountains beyond. The main floor of this fantasy suite is given over to a spacious and comfortable living room with an easy chair, a couch, a rocker, a desk, and an impressive floor-to-ceiling brick fireplace. There's also a full bathroom on this level.

Outside, a spacious deck beckons. Fortunately, we had a late dinner reservation and an extended happy hour during which the dark, craggy outline of the mountains lingered long after the sun had disappeared.

An oak-paneled stairway leads to the large bedroom where both the bed and the tiled spa tub boast private views of the vineyard. The bedroom offers a second handsome brick fireplace and another very cozy full bathroom. Both levels have televisions. This and other similarly styled suites carry weekend rates in the high $600 range.

For those who plan to spend more time in their bedroom than in the valley's tasting rooms, we recommend vineyard-view accommodations. Spacious vineyard-view rooms with king-sized feather beds, wood-burning fireplaces, and terraces are available in the high $400 range. Rooms with soft-sided outdoor terrace spa tubs are offered in the mid $500 range.

57

THE FACTS

Eighty-two rooms, suites, and lodges, each with private bath and deck; most have fireplaces. Amenities include comforters, bathrobes, bubblebath, and honor-bar refrigerators. Restaurants, bar, and lounges. Health spa equipped with whirlpool, lap pool, massage rooms, and fitness center. Tennis courts, swimming pool, golf course, and croquet lawn. Disabled access. Deluxe.

GETTING THERE

Follow Highway 29 north past Napa to St. Helena. In St. Helena, turn right on Pope Street. At the Silverado Trail, turn left, then make an immediate right on Howell Mountain Road; follow for a hundred yards and turn left on Meadowood Lane.

MEADOWOOD NAPA VALLEY
900 Meadowood Lane
St. Helena, CA 94574
Telephone: (707) 963-3646
Web site: www.meadowood.com

MEADOWOOD NAPA VALLEY

We may be hard-pressed to describe last night's dinner, but every visit to Meadowood remains a pleasant memory. Flaming crimson vineyards against a crisp, blue fall sky; the summer bike ride into St. Helena; those nattily dressed croquet players . . .

Meadowood has been a Napa Valley favorite of ours for years, yet we continue to encounter people who haven't had the pleasure of a weekend, a meal, or even a cocktail here. Tucked discreetly behind trees just above the Silverado Trail, the resort resists calling attention to itself. It's not marked by neon or any other conspicuous sign; you'll know you've arrived when you reach the security guard post. From there, the resort unfolds slowly as the road winds through the woods, past clusters of cottages, the swimming pool, tennis courts, and finally the property's central area.

While many hostelries offer only a few rooms that are eminently conducive to romance, we haven't discovered any accommodations at Meadowood that didn't measure up to our lovers' list of criteria.

Although the vastness of Meadowood can at first seem a bit intimidating (we followed a golf cart-driving bellman to our remote cottage), the wooded walkways and twisting lanes shed their mystery after a leisurely, get-acquainted stroll around the grounds.

At the northern end of the property is one of California's preeminent croquet lawns. The sight of well-heeled gentry, resplendent in crisp whites, playing in the shadow of Meadowood's Cape Cod architecture makes for a stunning, Gatsby-like scene, particularly on a sunny day.

The resort also offers swimming, tennis, golf, a well-equipped fitness facility, and the services of an on-site health spa.

ROOMS FOR ROMANCE

The resort has continued to grow in recent years. Recreational facilities have been expanded and many new guest-room buildings have sprouted throughout the wooded grounds.

Rates at Meadowood begin at around $600 per night for a Studio, a spacious accommodation that might feature a king-sized bed placed in an alcove, a sitting area, a wood-burning fireplace, a nice bathroom with a tub-and-shower combination, a terrace, and a view of the croquet lawns and golf fairways.

Lawnview rooms (mid $600 range) boast the above features as well as French doors that open to the croquet lawns. Treeline rooms with fireplaces (lower $700 range) comprise about five hundred square feet of romantic bliss, with separate bedrooms and sitting rooms, along with views of the wooded hillside environs. Hillside Terrace rooms (lower $800 range) are sumptuous hideaways with the above features in addition to soaking tubs.

THE FACTS

Five cottage rooms, each with private bath, refrigerator, CD player, television, ceiling fan, and gas fireplace; three rooms have whirlpool tubs for two. Complimentary full breakfast. No disabled access. Two-night minimum stay during weekends; three-night minimum during holiday periods. Moderate to deluxe.

GETTING THERE

From northbound Highway 101, drive past Healdsburg and exit at Dry Creek Road. Turn right on Dry Creek Road and left at the stoplight on Healdsburg Avenue. Drive one mile on Healdsburg Avenue (you'll see Simi Winery on your left) and turn right up the tree-lined drive to inn.

BELLE DE JOUR INN
16276 Healdsburg Avenue
Healdsburg, CA 95448
Telephone: (707) 431-9777
Web site: www.belledejourinn.com

BELLE DE JOUR INN

An Italianate-style farmhouse, home of longtime innkeepers Tom and Brenda Hearn, presides over this enclave of five tidy cottages, each equipped with the modern niceties conducive to a romantic getaway. The beds are even covered in crisp sheets dried by the sun.

Each morning, guests are invited into Tom and Brenda's house for breakfast, including cappuccino, latte, and espresso. Later in the day, the two (or even four) of you might want to schedule a romantic, chauffeured backroad or winery tour in the innkeepers' classic 1925 Star automobile.

ROOMS FOR ROMANCE

We particularly like the Carriage House (mid $300 range), where the entire second floor is a deluxe country suite with high vaulted ceilings, wood plank floors, and antique pine furniture. There's a CD player, a gas fireplace, and a reading nook made from redwood salvaged from the property's original barn. A view of the valley is offered from the king-sized four-poster bed and from the spa tub for two, which occupies its own alcove. There's also a separate shower.

The Terrace Room (upper $200 range) holds a king-sized plantation bed and a gas fireplace. A big spa tub for two sits at one end of the room under a window overlooking your private raised deck and an expanse of rolling, tree-studded countryside beyond. Roses bloom out front.

The Caretaker's Suite is another favorite. A king-sized, canopied bed dominates one end of this spacious room, which has hardwood floors and a sitting area with a love seat. A gas fireplace is close enough to warm your toes under the sheets. This room, which also boasts a whirlpool tub for two, is priced in the upper $200 range.

Atelier is a large sunny studio with a vaulted ceiling, a gas fireplace, a queen-sized, canopied bed, and a whirlpool tub for one. The Morning Hill Room has a French-door entry, a queen-sized bed, a gas fireplace, and a shower-and-steam unit in the bathroom. These two rooms are offered for around $200.

THE FACTS

Six rooms, each with fireplace, spa tub for two, surround-sound system, television, and balcony. Complimentary full breakfast served in first-floor restaurant at tables for two. Harmony Club Wine Bar and Restaurant. Disabled access. Deluxe.

GETTING THERE

From northbound Highway 12 in Sonoma, turn right at Sonoma Square on West Napa Street and proceed one block to First Street. Hotel faces the square near corner of West Napa and First Streets. Off-street hotel parking accessed via a narrow alley between theater and hotel.

LEDSON HOTEL
480 First Street
Sonoma, CA 95476
Telephone: (707) 996-9779
Web site: www.ledsonhotel.com

LEDSON HOTEL

As we have learned from experience, overnight accommodations in the Wine Country, like wine itself, are not all created equal. Fortunately, a great getaway destination, unlike a fine red wine, doesn't need years of aging to become extraordinary. Although the paint had barely dried at this exquisite new property when we spent a memorable night, the Ledson Hotel—at least by our judging—has already earned the title of Sonoma's "best in show."

The upscale hotel was crafted from the ground up by Sonoma County developer and farmer Steve Ledson, proprietor of the stately namesake winery near Kenwood known by many simply as the "castle." The hotel, which opened in 2003, hugs the vintage Sebastiani Theater facing picturesque Sonoma Square. Built to look old, the hotel sports a brick façade with wrought-iron flourishes and arched windows.

The richly appointed Harmony Club Wine Bar and Restaurant, which conjures images of a French bistro, occupies the first floor of the building. We dined at a charming sidewalk table during our warm-weather visit.

ROOMS FOR ROMANCE

Six guest rooms (around $400 each) comprise the entire second floor. Three face the square and three offer somewhat less inspiring but pleasant rear-facing courtyard views. All the guest quarters are intricately and finely crafted and lavishly appointed. Furnishings vary from room to room, but all the guest rooms share common features.

Our home for a night was the Winslow Room, where the small, marble-floored balcony proved a perfect vantage point from which to watch the world go by on bustling First Street and enjoy the leafy view of the charming town square directly across the street. The thick glass door and windows kept our room cozily quiet.

The room's centerpiece is a beautiful king-sized bed heaped with lush covers and pillows. The tall trees of Sonoma Square are visible from the bed. An ornate chandelier hangs above the bed, and there's a fireplace at your feet. A decadent spa tub for two sits at one end of the room in an elegant carved and mirrored alcove that looks as though it belongs in a royal palace. The richly marbled bathroom holds his-and-her vanities and a dark-green marble shower.

THE FACTS

Nineteen rooms, each with private bath and fireplace. Most with balconies. Complimentary full breakfast served in dining room at tables for two. Complimentary afternoon wine and refreshments. Communal spa. Bicycles available for guest use. Expensive.

GETTING THERE

Sonoma is about 45 miles north of San Francisco. Inn is located about two blocks south of Sonoma Square on the east side of Highway 12, which is called Broadway in Sonoma.

INN AT SONOMA

In Sonoma, history is all around. California's first commercial winery (Buena Vista) is thriving on the outskirts of town, Sonoma Square buildings dating back to the 1800s still welcome visitors, and the charming Victorian home of nineteenth century governor Mariano Vallejo has been lovingly preserved with support from proud townsfolk.

While we could have easily complemented the history theme by steering our readers to some of Sonoma's vintage inns, we opted to mix things up a bit, settling instead on a pair of getaway destinations that didn't exist until 2003.

Inn at Sonoma is the latest offering of the Four Sisters collection of West Coast inns that we've been recommending for the past decade. And the company's Sonoma property doesn't disappoint.

Set back a comfortable distance from bustling Broadway about three blocks from Sonoma Square, the inn is reached by a discreet driveway that's easy to miss if you're not paying attention. The unassuming, two-story inn is accented with chimneys and balconies, offering a hint of the features inside. Breakfast is served in a comfortable dining area on the first floor. The second floor boasts a welcoming communal outdoor spa and a sun deck.

The stores, galleries, coffee shops, and restaurants of Sonoma Square are a short walk away and will keep the two of you entertained for hours. The inn also provides bicycles for leisurely explorations of the town's charming neighborhoods. A number of intriguing wineries, including romantic Buena Vista, Ravenswood, and Gundlach Bundschu, are within a few minutes by car.

ROOMS FOR ROMANCE

Rooms ($200 to mid $200 range) are nicely decorated with wallpaper and appointed with fireplaces and comfortable chairs. Beds are king- or queen-sized. While all are nice, rooms 10, 11, and 12 have king-sized beds and larger balconies for soaking up the Sonoma sun.

INN AT SONOMA
630 Broadway
Sonoma, CA 95476
Telephone: (707) 939-1340
Web site: www.innatsonoma.com

DAYTIME DIVERSIONS

At **Stow Lake** (in the heart of **GOLDEN GATE PARK**), the two of you can rent a paddleboat for your own private cruise. The trail around the lake makes for a perfect quiet stroll and the park's venerable **Japanese Tea Garden** is another romantic spot. You'll follow delicate paths past a teahouse, a pagoda, and ponds and over intricate bridges. The cherry blossoms bloom in spring, making the Tea Garden a special place to visit in that season.

If you'd like to leave the crowds behind, board the **Tiburon Ferry** for a trip to **ANGEL ISLAND** in San Francisco Bay. You can bring your bikes on the ferry, and the island offers great private picnicking possibilities and enchanting city views.

TABLES FOR TWO

For a before- or after-dinner drink with a romantic **SAN FRANCISCO** view, try **Grandviews Lounge** on the thirty-sixth floor of the Grand Hyatt Hotel on Union Square, or **McCormick & Kuleto's** in Ghirardelli Square, which overlooks Aquatic Park, historic ships, the bay, and the Golden Gate Bridge. **The Compass Rose** at the Westin St. Francis Hotel on Union Square is another impressive lounge.

For dinner in the city, we can recommend **Aziza** (Moroccan), **Farallon** (seafood), **Clémentine** (French), **Jardinière** (California-French), **Kokkari** (Greek), **Boulevard** (Contemporary American), **Rose Pistola** (Italian), and **Acquerello** (Italian). Another top choice in San Francisco is **Aqua**, an elegant seafood restaurant located on California Street in the Financial District.

Mikayla, the restaurant at Casa Madrona (see listing), is a romantic favorite in **SAUSALITO**. Local innkeepers also recommend **Sushi Ran** and the venerable **Scoma's,** both in Sausalito. In **HALF MOON BAY,** we recommend **Cetrella** or **Pasta Moon.**

SAN FRANCISCO AND THE BAY AREA

THE FACTS

Fifty-four rooms, each with private bath, wood-burning fireplace, CD player, deep soaking tub, separate shower, and microwave. Complimentary continental breakfast served in lobby area, can be taken back to your room. Spa services. Swimming pool and communal spa. Fitness facility. Disabled access. Two-night minimum stay during holiday periods only. Expensive to deluxe.

GETTING THERE

From San Francisco, follow Interstate 280 south. Take the Highway 1/Pacifica exit. Follow Highway 1 south for approximately fifteen miles. Hotel is on the right, past the stoplight at Pillar Point Harbor. Hotel is about three miles north of downtown Half Moon Bay.

BEACH HOUSE AT HALF MOON BAY

In earlier editions of *Weekends for Two,* our Half Moon Bay picks leaned toward the quaint and old. Since we first profiled destinations in this coastal village, however, getaway alternatives have multiplied to include newer properties ranging from the sprawling and swanky Ritz Carlton to the smaller Beach House.

The latter, a three-story Cape Cod–cum-California structure, faces calm ocean waters and a narrow band of beach protected by a breakwater. The adjacent Pillar Point Harbor, which brims with pleasure boats and fishing crafts, can be seen from most rooms and is reached by a waterside walking path accessible from the hotel.

ROOMS FOR ROMANCE

For a romantic getaway, we recommend a room with a straight-on view of the ocean. Others (mid $200 range) have limited ocean views or none at all. Highway 1 is visible and audible from some rooms. Make sure to ask for a full-ocean-view room if that amenity is important to you.

We spent an enjoyable weekend in room 309 (mid $300 range), a third-floor, split-level penthouse room with a soaring ceiling. The lower half of the room consists of a cozy living area with a couch, a chair, a coffee table, a fireplace, and a granite-topped wet bar and kitchenette with a microwave oven and a stove. A sliding door and adjacent window frame an expansive view of the ocean and harbor. There's also a small balcony with two chairs. The raised sleeping area contains a king-sized bed and a desk. The bathroom holds a tub, a separate shower, and dual granite-topped sinks.

Ocean-view rooms on the lower floor (around $300) have patios that are slightly larger than the decks on the upper levels. The patios look out over a gentle landscaped bluff to the water.

The Half Moon Suite (high $300 range) is the inn's largest accommodation. Set above the pool and spa, the suite has both south- and west-facing decks and offers a nice southern coastal view.

BEACH HOUSE AT HALF MOON BAY
4100 Highway 1
Half Moon Bay, CA 94019
Telephone: (650) 712-0220;
toll-free: (800) 315-9366
Web site: www.beach-house.com

THE FACTS

Eighteen rooms, each with private bath, fireplace, and ocean-view deck. Complimentary full breakfast served at a communal table or delivered to your room. Complimentary afternoon tea. Disabled access. Two-night minimum stay during weekends, excluding Friday nights. Expensive to deluxe.

GETTING THERE

From Highway 1, twenty-six miles south of San Francisco and three miles north of Half Moon Bay, turn west onto Medio Avenue and follow to inn on the corner of Medio Avenue and Mirada Road.

CYPRESS INN ON MIRAMAR BEACH

407 Mirada Road
Half Moon Bay, CA 94019
Telephone: (650) 726-6002;
toll-free: (800) 832-3224
Web site: www.cypressinn.com

CYPRESS INN ON MIRAMAR BEACH

For the folks who run Cypress Inn on Miramar Beach, a beautiful but off-the-beaten-track location is a mixed blessing. Although they don't get too many drive-bys, say the innkeepers, guests who have discovered this contemporary hideaway enjoy not only blissful solitude but quick access (a dozen steps) to a five-mile stretch of white sandy beach.

ROOMS FOR ROMANCE

The main building offers El Sol (high $200 range), a sunny, lower-level corner room painted a bold yellow and decorated with wooden pillars and a tiled fireplace. On the second floor, El Viento beckons with a warm, pink theme and an ocean view.

Las Nubes (high $300 range), the third-floor penthouse suite, is the inn's largest and most romantic room, featuring magnificent, unobstructed ocean views, a large private deck, cushy sofas near the fireplace, and a spa tub for two. The bed even has an ocean view.

New to Cypress Inn since our last edition is the Lighthouse Building, our personal favorite, with six wonderfully romantic hideaways, most decorated in homage to California lighthouses. Surfing aficionados will no doubt covet The Maverick's room (upper $300 range), named after the famed surfing spot. This room offers a distant view of its namesake ocean point, and a sleek, custom-crafted surfboard by surfing legend Jeff Clarke hangs over the king-sized bed.

Sharing the second floor with Maverick's is Point Reyes (upper $300 range), which offers similar features including a spa tub for two, a king-sized bed, a gas fireplace, a sofa seating area, and great ocean views from the deck.

Even the nicely decorated Point Montara room (low $300 range), described as a partial ocean view accommodation, provides nice sea vistas from two windows.

A separate home behind the main building called the Beach House holds four rooms. The largest and most impressive is Dunes Beach (mid $300 range), a spacious second-floor corner room with a spa tub for two that offers a fireplace view. There's also a relaxing chaise set before a fireplace and a large deck with an ocean view. Readers should be aware that while most rooms in the Beach House building have ocean views, they also overlook the inn's parking area.

THE FACTS

Fifteen rooms and suites, each with private bath; most with fireplaces, some with tubs for two. Complimentary continental breakfast delivered to your room on a silver tray. Limited free parking. Disabled access. Two-night minimum stay during some weekends. Moderate to deluxe.

GETTING THERE

From the Bay Bridge, take the exit toward Mission Street/ Fell Street. Follow Highway 101 North signs. Take U.S. 101 North/Mission Street exit toward Van Ness Avenue and the Golden Gate Bridge. Turn right on Mission Street/Highway 101 North. Turn left on Hayes Street, left on Gough Street, right on Fell Street, and right on Steiner Street. Follow to Fulton Street.

ARCHBISHOP'S MANSION

One of our favorite romantic stories has its origins at this former home of Catholic archbishops. Moments after the infamous Northern California earthquake of 1989 that destroyed several San Francisco structures and violently shook many others, the Archbishop's Mansion innkeeper undertook a quick damage assessment outside. While she inspected the foundation, a couple opened their guest-room window and leaned their heads out. "Did you feel the earth move?" they asked, tongues planted firmly in cheek. "We did that!"

No doubt the inn's former residents and religious visitors would be more than a little shocked at the, er, activities that take place behind closed doors here these days, what with cozy fireplaces, canopied beds, and the like. Other than the name, not much remains to remind visitors of the inn's interesting past.

The spartan furnishings of yesteryear (the mansion was built a century ago and housed a succession of archbishops over a period of some forty years) have given way to a trove of beautiful objets d'art, antiques, and other pieces. Guest rooms, nicely updated while maintaining period charm, are also decorated with handsome furnishings dating back to the nineteenth century.

And don't forget to take a walk to the top of the hillside square for one of San Francisco's most often photographed views: the row of colorful Victorian "painted ladies" with the stunning city skyline looming above them.

ROOMS FOR ROMANCE

We sampled Traviata, a first-floor, two-room corner suite. The sunny sitting room, illuminated by several windows, holds a small fireplace with mirrored mantel and several antiques. Accessible only through the bathroom, the bedroom holds a king-sized bed.

The Gypsy Baron (high $200 range) is the inn's honeymoon suite, with a large fireplace and tub for two. Double spa tubs are also found in two more rooms, Der Rosenkavalier and Romeo and Juliet (low $200 range). In the top-of-the line Don Giovanni Suite (high $300 range), originally the archbishop's bedroom, guests are treated to a large parlor, two fireplaces, and an antique bed from a French castle. The second-floor Carmen Suite (high $200 range) features an expansive bathroom with a clawfoot tub and its own fireplace.

Romantics on a budget may sample a couple of cozy rooms with canopied beds priced in the low to mid $100 range.

ARCHBISHOP'S MANSION
1000 Fulton Street
San Francisco, CA 94117
Telephone: (415) 563-7872;
toll-free: (800) 543-5820
Web site: www.thearchbishopsmansion.com

THE FACTS

Forty-nine rooms, each with private bath, television, and videocassette and CD player. Many with kitchenettes. Complimentary continental breakfast. Complimentary afternoon refreshments. Video and CD lending library. Complimentary indoor parking. Access to nearby fitness center. Pet-friendly rooms. Smoking is permitted in some rooms. Moderate to expensive.

GETTING THERE

From San Francisco's downtown Financial District, drive west on California Street and follow uphill to Pacific Heights. Hotel is at corner of California and Presidio Streets.

Finally, our wish for a comfortable boutique hotel in San Francisco's swanky Pacific Heights neighborhood has been granted. For San Francisco visitors who prefer to be a bit removed from the madding downtown crowd, this small hotel fills the bill.

The Laurel is part of the delightfully eclectic Joie de Vivre Hospitality group, which also manages or owns other hotels we're sharing with readers for the first time in this revised edition of *Weekends for Two*.

ROOMS FOR ROMANCE

Guest rooms, which are spread over three floors, are decorated in a bold, contemporary, angular fashion. The decor, while not luxurious, is colorful and comfortably hip.

Large and affordable by San Francisco standards, rooms here have either two double beds or one king-sized bed. For a romantic getaway, we recommend the City View King rooms (upper $100 range including on-site parking). These spacious accommodations have sitting areas, desks, kitchenettes, and large windows with sweeping city views. Bathrooms, on the small side, are nicely equipped with marble sinks and tub and-shower combinations.

All rooms have a CD player and a television, and the inn provides a lending library of music and films. Nonsmoking rooms are available. This hotel describes itself as pet-friendly.

THE LAUREL INN

444 Presidio Avenue
San Francisco, CA 94115
Telephone: (415) 567-8467
Web site: www.thelaurelinn.com

NOB HILL LAMBOURNE
725 Pine Street
San Francisco, CA 94108
Telephone: (415) 433-2287;
toll-free: (800) 274-8466
Web site: www.nobhilllambourne.com

THE FACTS

Twenty rooms and suites, each with private bath, kitchen-ette, and deep soaking tub. Complimentary continental breakfast served in parlor area. Complimentary evening wine reception. Massage treatment room. Valet parking for additional charge. Hotel uses chemical-free cleaning products. Expensive.

GETTING THERE

The hotel is located on Pine Street, two blocks from the top of Nob Hill and three blocks north of Union Square, between Powell and Stockton Streets. The Powell Street cable car line is a half-block away.

NOB HILL LAMBOURNE

In these days of specialty travel, there are destinations designed to appeal to just about every individual taste. "Our niche," says the general manager of Nob Hill Lambourne, "is healthy guests." Billed as "a hotel for the mind, body, and soul—a place where wellness and hospitality blend . . ." Nob Hill Lambourne promises a striking contrast to the big city that bustles outside its doors. It's a brand promise that has made this a favorite destination not only among business travelers but among weekending couples seeking a tranquil place to stay in the City-by-the-Bay.

The inn's theme is demonstrated in a number of ways. Nob Hill Lambourne provides exercise machines in its suites, in-room honor bars offering homeopathic remedies, and massages. In addition, guests receive energy supplements at evening turn-down, and the housekeepers use nonchemical cleaning supplies.

ROOMS FOR ROMANCE

Boasting a downtown-convenient Nob Hill location just three blocks from Union Square and literally steps to the Powell Street cable car line, Nob Hill Lambourne began life as an apartment complex. Warmly lit, its rooms retain touches like small decks, interesting angles, and kitchenettes. Accommodations are clean, fresh, and traditional in style. Large desks, high-speed data ports, and fax machines provide a hint about the workweek clientele.

For romantic getaways, our top recommendation goes to the inn's three suites. We spent a night in the Lola Montez Suite (low to mid $200 range), a spacious and quiet ground-floor hideaway at the rear of the building. The living room holds a couch, two wing chairs, and a table. A small, dark-wood armoire hides a television, and an office alcove holds a desk. There's also a tiny kitchenette with a two-burner stove, a sink, a refrigerator, and a microwave. A sliding door in the living room opens to a small deck in a not-so-private inner court area. The separate bedroom has a queen-sized bed and an exercise machine. The bathroom holds a deep tub for one.

The Deluxe Queen rooms (high $100 range) are nice quarters as well, and some feature bay windows. However, these rooms are smaller and offer limited seating options for couples.

THE FACTS

Twenty-six rooms, each with private bath and gas fireplace. Complimentary full buffet breakfast served at tables for two in the dining room and patio or delivered to your room for an extra charge. Complimentary afternoon cookies and evening wine and refreshments. Fitness room. Valet parking. No disabled access. Moderate to deluxe.

GETTING THERE

From Highway 101 (Van Ness Avenue), turn east on Bush Street. The inn is between Mason and Taylor Streets, two and a half blocks from Union Square and one and a half blocks to Powell Street cable car line.

THE WHITE SWAN INN

Its location may be downtown San Francisco, but The White Swan Inn draws its inspiration from merry old England. The inn's amenities, from the English-style library and British collectibles on display to the handsome Old World antiques in rich, warm woods, might just make you feel more like a tourist in London than in the City-by-the-Bay. It's a comfortable base from which to enjoy all that San Francisco has to offer.

ROOMS FOR ROMANCE

Rooms at The White Swan are differentiated not so much by amenities and decor—they're each equipped with a gas fireplace, a wet bar, a private bathroom, and attractive furnishings—as by bed and room size.

Room 44 (mid to high $100 range) on the fourth floor is a queen-bed room. It faces the side of the hotel and features a nice window seat, sans view. The bathroom is small but manages to include all the necessities.

While we found the queen-bed rooms adequate in size, the king-bed rooms, offered for about $20 more, are larger. For instance, room 47 has a separate dressing area with a sink. The windows in this sunny room comprise almost an entire wall (with no view to speak of). This and the other king-bed rooms that have numbers ending with a 6 or 7 all face the back of the property and are among the most quiet.

The inn also offers honeymoon suites (high $200 range) with canopied beds and refrigerators stocked with complimentary refreshments.

THE WHITE SWAN INN

845 Bush Street
San Francisco, CA 94108
Telephone: (415) 755-1755;
toll-free: (800) 999-9570
Web site: www.jdvhospitality.com

THE FACTS

Thirty-four rooms and suites, each with private bath; sixteen have fireplaces and four have tubs for two. Restaurant. Spa. Complimentary continental breakfast served in restaurant or in your room. Disabled access. Two-night minimum stay during weekends. Moderate to deluxe.

GETTING THERE

From Highway 101 north, exit at Alexander Avenue and follow to Bridgeway. From Highway 101 south, take Marin/Sausalito exit to Bridgeway.

CASA MADRONA HOTEL
801 Bridgeway
Sausalito, CA 94965
Telephone: (415) 332-0502
Web site: www.casamadrona.com

CASA MADRONA HOTEL

Choosing a romantic room at Casa Madrona is like making a selection from the menu of a four-star restaurant. It'll make you hungry and you'll definitely have trouble deciding. To complicate matters, every time we visit, the menu seems to get longer.

Since our last Casa Madrona encounter, the hotel, which drapes over a Sausalito hillside, has doubled in size, and the additions are as dazzling as the original rooms that enchanted us more than a decade ago.

ROOMS FOR ROMANCE

The Superior rooms (mid $200 range) are located primarily in the original mansion that for many years comprised the entire inn. The Garden- and Courtyard-View rooms (high $200 range) are found in the original hotel building and in a more recent addition where rooms boast a more contemporary feel, more luxurious bathrooms, and deep soaking tubs. The Bayview rooms (mid $300 range) are our favorites, offering romantic Richardson's Bay vistas. Some of these have private balconies and patios.

Among the dozen rooms in the manor house is La Salle, decorated in a French country style and complemented by a dual spa tub. The Belle Vista Suite offers a romantic San Francisco skyline view and a freestanding tub for two in the living room.

The gabled and balconied rooms of New Casa sweep artfully down the hillside below the manor house. Rooms here are modern and come in many shapes, sizes, and styles. In Kathmandu, huge cushions encourage lounging and tiny nooks invite exploring. A fireplace and tub for two complete this room.

Also worth noting are the Rose Chalet with its pine furniture, separate bed alcove, fireplace, and deck; the Renoir Room, where guests luxuriate in a clawfoot tub surrounded by a garden mural. There's also a window seat, a fireplace, and a deck from which to enjoy a spectacular bay view.

THE FACTS

Thirty rooms, each with private bath and tub for two; most with wood-burning or gas fireplaces. Complimentary continental breakfast served at communal table, tables for two, or in your room. Complimentary wine served in the evening. Disabled access. Two-night minimum stay during weekends and holiday periods. Expensive to deluxe.

GETTING THERE

From Highway 101 north of San Francisco, take the Alexander Avenue exit and drive one mile (Alexander becomes Bridgeway). Turn right on El Portal and follow to inn. Sausalito is about a twenty-minute (non-rush-hour) drive from San Francisco.

THE INN ABOVE TIDE
30 El Portal
Sausalito, CA 94965
Telephone: (415) 332-9535
Web site: www.innabovetide.com

82

THE INN ABOVE TIDE

Built years ago as a luxury apartment complex whose residents included Hollywood luminaries like Sam Peckinpah and Clint Eastwood, the three-story, shingled Inn Above Tide sits on pilings directly over San Francisco Bay. A $3.5 million conversion a decade or so ago created this idyllic overnight destination, where every room offers enchanting panoramic bay and city views. It's arguably the best view of the city you'll find from a Bay Area guest room.

The Red and White Fleet and Golden Gate ferry both dock next door to the inn, and a number of restaurants and nightspots are within walking distance. If the two of you can't tear yourselves away from this romantic environment for dinner, the inn has an arrangement with a local restaurant that will bring supper to your room.

ROOMS FOR ROMANCE

The Superior rooms (mid $200 range) are quite superior indeed. These have either king-sized beds or two double beds, and they feature sweeping bay views and gas fireplaces. All bathrooms have tubs big enough for two, and furnishings are plush and comfortable. Rooms with corner windows providing even more impressive bay vistas are offered in the upper $300 range.

The Queen Deluxe rooms (upper $200 range) offer private bay-view decks along with fireplaces and love seats. Deluxe rooms with king-sized beds and private decks command tariffs of around $300.

Nicer still are the Grand Deluxe rooms (around $400) with a larger sweep of bay-view windows and floor-to-ceiling fireplaces. We visited during a quiet midweek period and sampled room 101 in this category. We particularly enjoyed lounging on our deck, enjoying a glass of champagne, and watching the late-afternoon ferryboat disgorge business-suited San Francisco workers as they arrived home from the city across the bay. The panorama from here is second to none, and takes in the exclusive enclave of Belvedere as well as San Francisco Bay, Angel Island, various East Bay cities, and the Bay Bridge.

THE FACTS

Twenty-three rooms, each with private bath and fireplace. Most with balconies. Complimentary continental breakfast served in your room. Complimentary evening wine. Free parking nearby. No minimum stay. Expensive to deluxe.

GETTING THERE

From Highway 101 north of the Golden Gate Bridge, take Tiburon Boulevard/East Blithedale Avenue exit. Turn right at traffic light on Tiburon Boulevard. Drive approximately four miles to Tiburon. Turn right at Main Street and follow one-half block to inn on left.

WATERS EDGE

Until fairly recently, weekend encounters with this ultra-exclusive community were primarily of the fleeting kind. A typical Tiburon visit afforded opportunities for shopping, bicycling, and dining, but overnight options were decidedly limited. That all changed not long ago with the arrival of Waters Edge, a small, charming boutique hotel that overhangs the bay, serving up sumptuous Angel Island and San Francisco views along with luxuriously cozy rooms.

Operated by the quirky Joie de Vivre Hospitality group of small hotels, Waters Edge has a physical plan reminiscent of East Coast seaside architecture. The building rests on a historic dock immediately adjacent to the landing for Angel Island ferryboats. The quaint shops and restaurants of Tiburon are just steps away.

ROOMS FOR ROMANCE

The View King rooms (around $300) are equipped with king-sized beds, fireplaces, and comfy chaises and chairs. Walls are muted in color, the sleek contemporary furnishings in dark tones. From the small decks provided with most guest rooms, visitors savor the sound of the gently lapping bay waters and the calming sight of nautical comings and goings.

The hotel's two Grand King suites (around $400) are our picks for a very special getaway. These luxurious rooms hover over the water and feature a sitting area with love seat, a bay-view window, and a fireplace that's visible from both the bed and sitting area. Both have semiprivate view decks.

In the morning, the two of you will be treated to an extensive continental breakfast and newspaper delivered to your room. The inn's communal waterside deck offers stunning views of Angel Island and San Francisco.

WATERS EDGE
25 Main Street
Tiburon, CA 94920
Telephone: (415) 789-5999;
toll-free: (877) 789-5999
Web site: www.marinhotels.com

DAYTIME DIVERSIONS

While everyone homes in on the shops of CARMEL, too many folks pass up the chance to stroll the beautiful, white-sand beach along Carmel Bay. Don't miss it, especially on a sunny day. The beach is only a short walk from the heart of the village.

In MONTEREY, Northern California's other Fisherman's Wharf is crammed with little open-air markets that display a variety of fresh catches. The district is within walking distance of the Old Monterey Inn (see listing).

Visitors to Cannery Row's world-famous Monterey Bay Aquarium shouldn't overlook the paved pedestrian and bike path that links Cannery Row with Pacific Grove. Surrey rentals are available along the seaside path. Despite the sometimes heavy foot and cycle traffic, it's one of the most romantic promenades you'll ever take.

Near CARMEL, the romantically medieval Tor House, built by poet Robinson Jeffers, is still in use by the family but is open for weekend tours with advance reservations.

TABLES FOR TWO

In PACIFIC GROVE, our innkeepers recommend the White House on Lighthouse Avenue and Fandango's on Seventeenth Street.

In the village of Carmel, the two of you will surely enjoy Anton and Michel, Casanova, or Flying High.

Ventana's highly rated on-site restaurant (see listing; early reservations advised) is accessible to resort guests via a winding, romantic path through the Big Sur forest. Trailside lights guide you and other hand-holding couples back to your rooms after dinner.

THE CENTRAL COAST

THE FACTS

Sixty rooms and suites, each with private bath, refrigerator, and videocassette or DVD player; most with fireplaces; several with private outdoor spas. Complimentary continental breakfast and afternoon wine and cheese. Restaurant, on-site store. Pools, sauna, Japanese-style baths, fitness room, spa services, guided hikes. Disabled access. Two-night minimum stay during weekends. Deluxe.

GETTING THERE

Ventana is located 28 miles south of the last traffic light in Carmel just off coastal Highway 1. The drive from Monterey takes about forty-five minutes.

VENTANA
Highway 1
Big Sur, CA 93920
Telephone: (408) 667-2331;
toll-free: (800) 628-6500
Web site: www.ventanainn.com

VENTANA

Granted, the sight and sound of surf breaking just outside your window is pretty special, especially to big-city folk. But there's nothing like a fifty-mile, tree-and-sea view from high above the ocean when it comes to sensual stimulus.

Encouraged by a couple of friends who termed Ventana a hedonistic hideaway, we booked a room a decade ago to celebrate a special birthday. Since then it's become our "special birthday place." The inn and its incomparable setting are simply spectacular.

Ventana's sixty guest rooms are spread among some 240 acres in a dozen single- and two-story units of weathered cedar. Accommodations are connected by footpaths that wind through a mountain meadow ringed by redwood, oak, and bay laurel trees. Another footpath, romantically lit at night, leads through the forest to Ventana's renowned Cielo restaurant a short stroll away.

Because of the privacy-sensitive layout of the complex (not to mention the indoor entertainment options), you're likely to feel alone, even when the inn is booked solid. The largest gathering of guests—some dressed comfortably in robes—is often found in the late afternoon, sampling a sumptuous, complimentary wine-and-cheese buffet on the inn's terrace. Continental breakfast is also served communally, but most prefer to dine in their rooms.

ROOMS FOR ROMANCE

Room 53, The Cottage (mid $800 range), is situated at the rear of Ventana's property, overlooking seemingly endless miles of forest. We stayed here and spent much of our time relaxing in our private, deck-mounted spa tub under the highest reaches of a grand oak.

Another visit found us in the fabulous room 4, a Vista hot tub suite that's a favorite among celebrity couples. This hideaway features a large wooden hillside deck with a private spa tub overlooking the ocean, and inside we were treated to a corner fireplace, a sitting area, and a king-sized bed. The decadent bathroom is appointed with a deep tub set under an ocean-view window and a larger shower with a floor-to-ceiling window framing an ocean vista.

Ventana's least expensive guest rooms with adjoining view decks start in the low $400 range. Rooms with fireplaces run from the upper $400 range to the mid $500 range. Some of the resort's most sublime accommodations are those with private hot tubs on the outside and fireplaces inside (from the low $700 range). Every room has either a balcony or a patio, and most have ocean vistas.

Even if an expensive suite is out of reach, you'll still have access to communal Japanese-style hot baths, a swimming pool, a sauna, and a sun-deck. Clothing-optional areas are also provided.

A final note: although check-in isn't until 4:00 P.M., Ventana's liberal 1:00 P.M. checkout time is the most generous of all our destinations. You'll want to savor every last moment.

THE FACTS

Twenty-four rooms, each with private bath, refrigerator, and gas fireplace. Complimentary full breakfast served in dining room. Complimentary afternoon wine and refreshments. Disabled access. Moderate to expensive.

GETTING THERE

From Highway 1 at Carmel, take Ocean Avenue exit; turn left on Junipero and drive two blocks to inn.

COBBLESTONE INN

Junipero between Seventh and Eighth
(P.O. Box 3185)
Carmel, CA 93921
Telephone: (831) 625-5222
Web site: www.foursisters.com

COBBLESTONE INN

Once upon a time, this was just another plain-Jane motel. But with the addition of a distinctive stone façade, fresh country decor, and a few other touches of "Carmelization," the Cobblestone has become one of the village's most romantic retreats.

The inn is set in a neighborhood with a mix of homes and businesses, and it's only two blocks from the heart of Carmel village. A walk of about eight blocks will bring you to Carmel's glorious white-sand beach.

ROOMS FOR ROMANCE

The inn's designated honeymoon suite is room 27, a particularly sunny hideaway (mid $200 range) featuring a king-sized four-poster bed and a recessed sitting area under the windows. The bath has a tub-and-shower combination. Only guests staying in this room are treated to breakfast in bed.

Room 26 is another bright room, decked out in style to match the inn's pervasive English country theme. But this one is priced more moderately, in the mid $100 range. One of the favorites is room 18 (high $100 range), a sunny corner room with a king-sized bed and a sitting area with a sofa.

The rooms, each equipped with a stocked refrigerator and a gas fireplace, are arranged in a horseshoe shape around a well-tended slate court-yard dotted with flower planters and small tables.

THE FACTS

*Ten rooms and suites, nine with fireplaces. Complimentary
full breakfast served at a large communal table, in the
garden, or in your room. In-room massages available. No
disabled access. Two-night minimum stay during weekends;
three-night minimum during holidays. Expensive to deluxe.*

GETTING THERE

*Monterey is 115 miles south of San Francisco on Highway 1.
From Pacific Street near the city's historic section, head
east on Martin Street. The inn is situated in a residential
area and is marked by a small sign on the right side of
Martin Street.*

OLD MONTEREY INN
500 Martin Street
Monterey, CA 93940
Telephone: (831) 375-8284
Web site: www.oldmontereyinn.com

OLD MONTEREY INN

We had a hunch we were in for a treat after the second or third pass along Martin Street searching for the Old Monterey Inn. In our experience, the harder an inn is to find, the more special it will be.

Our theory was confirmed when we finally spotted the tiny sign in a tree and entered the wooded grounds of what in our opinion ranks as Monterey Peninsula's preeminent inn.

The Tudor-style, craftsman estate in which longtime proprietor Ann Swett raised six children contains ten guest rooms, each with private bath and each offering a different guest experience, thanks to Ann's decorating flourishes.

Depending on your mood (or the unpredictable Monterey weather), complimentary full breakfast is served either in the impressive dining room, outdoors in the garden, or in your room. Although we'd planned to dine under our warm, down comforter, the morning sun drew us into the garden with several other guests for a memorable breakfast of waffles, whipped cream, and berries.

ROOMS FOR ROMANCE

Tattershall (upper $200 range) welcomes guests with its French toile decor. Morning sun floods this room, which features a luxurious queen-sized bed to warm your hearts and a pretty tiled fireplace to warm your toes.

One of the main house's most private hideaways is Dovecote (upper $200 range), a rear-facing third-floor room with an English theme. A fireplace, queen-sized bed, window seat, and skylight are among the thoughtful features here.

We were particularly intrigued by Stoneleigh (mid $300 range), a Carriage House retreat that pampers guests with a wood-burning fireplace at the foot of the draped bed and a romantic bath with tumbled marble pebbles surrounding a spa tub for two. This room has a private entrance.

Our home for a night was the Garden Cottage (mid $400 range), a spacious suite with a cozy sitting room, a fireplace, and a step-up bedroom. The shuttered windows frame an elevated view filtered through limbs of twisting oaks in the garden beyond. A large spa tub for two set under a skylight completes this romantic package.

New since our last visit is the Mayfield Suite (around $400), where the centerpiece is an in-room spa tub for two. This room features a king-sized bed, a windowed sitting area, and a fireplace.

Each room at Old Monterey Inn boasts a plush feather bed, a down duvet, upscale linens, thick towels, and terry robes. Although rooms have televisions and videocassette players, they're equipped with phones for outgoing calls only. Messages received through the inn's main phone are promptly delivered to your room. Reasons Ann, "The phone always seems to ring at the wrong time, so this way the guest has control." An innkeeper after our own heart.

THE FACTS

Forty-two rooms, each with private bath and wood-burning fireplace. Half of the rooms have bay views with window seats. Complimentary continental breakfast and morning newspaper delivered to your room. Disabled access. Two-night minimum stay during most weekends. Expensive to deluxe.

GETTING THERE

Monterey is about 120 miles from San Francisco International Airport. From Highway 1, take the Monterey exit and drive west. Turn left on Del Monte Boulevard; veer right at the fork. Turn right on Hoffman Avenue and left onto Cannery Row. The inn is at the heart of Cannery Row on the bay side of the street.

SPINDRIFT INN
652 Cannery Row
Monterey, CA 93940
Telephone: (831) 646-8900;
toll-free: (800) 841-1879
Web site: www.spindriftinn.com

SPINDRIFT INN

For those expecting to experience the Cannery Row of John Steinbeck's literature, a trip down the narrow row during a busy weekend can be a somewhat disappointing experience. Tour buses hog the parking lots, tourists clog the streets, and many of the original buildings have been replaced by stucco façades.

During the evening and early morning hours, however, the picture changes completely. When the cars and tourists leave, the fog sometimes settles in, enveloping the smells and sounds of Cannery Row as immortalized by Steinbeck's pen. In the early morning, lapping waves and a distant foghorn are all that can be heard. These precious hours offer an enchanting taste of what the fabled street must have been like when the fish outnumbered the tourists.

Despite its modernization, Cannery Row is still a magical getaway for lovers, especially when savored from the Spindrift Inn. Built on the beach, on the site of an old hotel, the inn offers considerable serenity despite its location at the heart of the row.

Spindrift is just down the street from the Monterey Bay Aquarium and a short jaunt from Fisherman's Wharf. A biking/walking path hugs the coastline connecting Cannery Row with quaint Pacific Grove and the wharf.

ROOMS FOR ROMANCE

Although our room faced Cannery Row, we could also see the bay thanks to expansive corner windows. With the exception of views, the rooms here are similar. Each one includes a wood-burning fireplace, traditional furnishings, a canopied and draped feather bed, and a comforter. A remote-controlled television is hidden in an armoire. The marble baths feature brass fixtures and a second telephone. Rooms feature either window seats or balconies.

Rates at Spindrift Inn run from the high $100 range to the low $400 range. The most expensive are those facing the bay. Bay-facing corner rooms, which offer dazzling views, are most coveted by traveling romantics.

THE FACTS

Eleven rooms, seven with private baths; six with fireplaces. Complimentary full breakfast served buffet-style or delivered to your room at extra charge. No minimum stay requirement. Moderate to expensive.

GETTING THERE

From Highway 1, take Highway 68 west to Pacific Grove. Highway 68 becomes Forest Avenue; continue on Forest Avenue to the beach; turn right on Ocean View Boulevard to inn, at the corner of Fifth Street.

GREEN GABLES INN
301 Ocean View Boulevard
Pacific Grove, CA 93950
Telephone: (408) 375-2095;
toll-free: (800) 722-1774
Web site: www.foursisters.com

GREEN GABLES INN

We learn a lot about an inn from the guest book. While many innkeepers rely on new clientele to stay busy, the guest register at Green Gables Inn features names of travelers who have sampled every room. On any given morning, the breakfast table will likely host at least a couple or two who are paying a return visit. It's this kind of romantic reputation that has made the Green Gables among the most popular of our featured destinations for over a decade.

An architectural showstopper in its own right, the inn is doubly spectacular given its locale. If the water were any closer, you could fish from your window. Only a two-lane road separates this lovely Queen Anne Victorian from Monterey Bay, and most of the distinctive gabled rooms have dramatic views of the sea or coastline.

ROOMS FOR ROMANCE

Among returning guests, the most requested room (even though it shares a bath) is Balcony (mid $100 range), on the second floor. One of the particularly appealing attractions of this room, in addition to the ocean view, is the step-down sun porch with daybed. There's no need to draw the drapes for privacy, since neither the adjacent street nor the bike path is visible from your bed. Just enjoy the spectacular view.

Another popular room, Chapel (mid $100 range), features old mahogany, an open-beam ceiling, and a step-up window seat. It shares a pair of easily accessible bathrooms with three other rooms.

Jennifer's Room, which does have its own bath with shower, has a huge wall-length window and a window seat.

The vast Lacy Suite is the inn's most expensive accommodation, priced in the mid $200 range. It holds a queen-sized canopied bed, a private bath with antique tub, a huge armoire that covers almost an entire wall, and a sitting room with a gas fireplace. The sitting room and bedchamber are separated by a pretty sliding door. The suite does not have an ocean view and is located directly off the living room.

Elsewhere in the main house is Garret, which we found a bit too small. It also shares a bath.

While the fairy-tale façade of the main house can prove hard to resist, many guests head for the separate three-level Carriage House (mid $200 range). Rooms here each have a partial ocean view, a king-sized bed, a gas fireplace, and a private bath. These rooms are spacious but do lack some of the antique charm of the main house.

The Green Gables is part of the Four Sisters collection of small hotels and inns. Whichever room you choose, you'll be greeted by one of the Four Sisters trademarks: a cuddly teddy bear placed somewhere in your chambers.

THE FACTS

*Fourteen rooms, each with private bath and bay/ocean/coastal
view. Complimentary full breakfast served in parlor area.
Afternoon refreshments. Disabled access. Two-night minimum stay during weekends; three-night minimum during
certain holiday periods. Moderate to deluxe.*

GETTING THERE

*From Highway 1, take Highway 68 west to Pacific Grove.
Highway 68 becomes Forest Avenue; stay on Forest Avenue
to Ocean View Boulevard and turn right; follow for two
blocks to inn.*

SEVEN GABLES INN

555 Ocean View Boulevard
Pacific Grove, CA 93950
Telephone: (831) 372-4341
Web site: www.pginns.com

SEVEN GABLES INN

Arguably California's most beautiful Victorian inn, Seven Gables is the place you've always fantasized about. Relaxing in the front yard on a sunny afternoon, we watched car after car slow to gawking speed when passing this classic beauty on Ocean View Boulevard. Even though we were only there for a night, I felt like the guy at the prom with the prettiest girl.

Thanks to the inn's longtime proprietors, the Flatley family, those gingerbread-laden, gabled rooms that for generations were only enjoyed by the home's owners may now be savored by the rest of us. It's true that the stately exterior, immortalized in VISA commercials, sets lofty expectations. But the interior more than lives up to them: the public rooms that greet arriving guests are ostentatious displays of Victoriana, with gilded fixtures, museum-quality antiques, and ornately patterned rugs.

The period theme is carried into the guest rooms, which boast appointments like down-filled couches, inlaid tables and sideboards, antique prints, nine-foot-high armoires, and velvet-covered chairs.

Views from many of the inn's rooms are postcard-quality. Although you'll rue the setting of the sun bringing down the curtain on this scene, the night kicks the other senses into high gear. The smell of the sea and sounds of crashing surf at night lulled us for hours.

Breakfast at Seven Gables, which includes a hot entrée, is a convivial, sit-down affair in the inn's ornate dining room.

ROOMS FOR ROMANCE

The room most coveted by traveling romantics is Cypress (mid $300 range), a second-floor room in the Guest House that boasts a 180-degree view of the ocean and bay. This idyllic retreat is appointed with a canopied king-sized bed, a huge armoire, two antique stained-glass windows, a couch, and a sitting area. The bathroom has a tub-and-shower combination.

The very private Gable Room (high $200 range) is located on the third floor at the tippety top of the main house and boasts lots of interesting angles as well as a nice-sized bathroom with a shower.

The largest of the inn's seven gables is found behind the door of the Bellevue Room (low $300 range), where an elegant chandelier hangs above the bay-view sitting area. This room has a draped queen-sized bed.

The renovated Carriage House cottage (mid $200 range) has a bay window and window seat overlooking the garden and ocean. This quaint retreat is furnished with a gas fireplace and a canopied queen-sized bed.

If there's no vacancy at Seven Gables, we can also recommend the Grand View Inn, a sister property located just next door (and featured in *Weekends for Two in the Wine Country*).

THE FACTS

Forty-five bungalows, villas, and homes, each with wet bar, spa tub for two, flat-screen television, DVD and CD player, and patio. Restaurants, bar, and room service. Golf course, swimming pool, cigar room, full-service spa, fitness room. Disabled access. Two-night minimum stay during weekends. Deluxe.

GETTING THERE

CordeValle is located thirty miles south of San Jose and forty-five miles north of the Monterey Peninsula. From Highway 101, take the San Martin Avenue exit and drive west. Turn left on Monterey Road. Turn right on Highland Avenue and follow to resort.

THE LODGE AT CORDEVALLE

Whether you both enjoy golf or just one of you pursues the game, a full-service golf resort can be a great choice for a weekend getaway for two. For the enthusiast, there's a course just outside the door, and the golf widow or widower has a variety of indulgent activities from which to choose. And at the end of the day you've got each other, in a romantic setting free from domestic diversions.

The Lodge at CordeValle fills the bill perfectly. This impressive new golf resort, set among oak-studded hills not far from Monterey Bay, was developed by the same folks who brought us the enchanting Auberge du Soleil in the Wine Country (see separate listing). Traveling romantics won't be disappointed.

In addition to enjoying first-tier accommodations, overnight couples have plenty to keep them busy. Amenities here include a championship course designed by Robert Trent Jones, a full-service spa with a variety of treatments, a fitness room, a swimming pool, a restaurant and bar, and even a cigar room. A round of golf, including cart, runs in the high $100 range for overnight guests who are not club members.

ROOMS FOR ROMANCE

The resort's twenty-eight bungalows (mid $400 to mid $500 range) represent the lion's share of accommodations, and they're a perfect choice for traveling romantics. Offering seven hundred square feet of living space, these spacious hideaways feature craftsman-style touches along with king-sized beds, upscale linens, fireplaces with seating areas, comfy chairs, and desks. Each has a satellite-connected, flat-screen television and a DVD and CD player. Well-appointed bathrooms feature double vanities, spa tubs, and separate showers. Outside is a private patio with an oak-lined fairway view.

Five ultra-spacious and decadently romantic villas ($800 range) are set against a hillside and offer nicely appointed separate living rooms and bedrooms, each of which has an expansive fairway and hillside view. The villas also feature private outdoor spas.

THE LODGE AT CORDEVALLE
1 CordeValle Club Drive
San Martin, CA 95046
Telephone: (408) 695-4500;
toll-free: (877) 255-2626
Web site: www.cordevalle.com

THE FACTS

Forty-room main lodge plus numerous cabins and "canvas cabins." Cabins share bath facilities. Café, general store. Communal hot tub, picnic area, spa services. Mountain bike rentals, guided hikes and workshops, horseback riding, kayaking. Saturday barbeque. Disabled access. Moderate to expensive.

GETTING THERE

The resort is located about twenty-five miles south of Half Moon Bay and twenty-five miles north of Santa Cruz. From Highway 1 near Año Nuevo State Reserve and south of Pescadero, drive east on Rossi Road to resort.

COSTANOA COASTAL LODGE AND CAMP
2001 Rossi Road
Pescadero, CA 94060
Telephone: (650) 879-1100;
toll-free: (877) 262-7848
Web site: www.costanoa.com

COSTANOA COASTAL LODGE AND CAMP

In more than a decade of romantic travels that have taken us from coast to coast, nowhere have we found a range of accommodations to rival Costanoa. Whether your travel taste runs to a canvas tent or to the conveniences and comforts of a lodge room, you'll find what you're looking for at this unique getaway destination.

Although Costanoa is described as a luxury camping resort, it's a place that defies simple descriptors. It's part luxury lodge, part cozy traditional cabins, and part upscale canvas tents. There are even spaces for recreational vehicles and places for the two of you to pitch your own tents. The resort also provides guests with a well-stocked general store and a variety of organized activities ranging from Native American storytelling and personal growth workshops to naturalist-led hikes and stargazing walks.

ROOMS FOR ROMANCE

The attractive main lodge houses comfortable and nicely appointed rooms including private bathrooms. The Lodge Premium rooms (mid $200 range) on the second floor have view balconies, king-sized beds, raised fireplaces in stone surrounds, and oval-shaped tubs for two with sliding doors that open to the bedroom. The bathrooms also have separate showers.

We never thought we'd be describing tents to our readers, but Costanoa's more rustic accommodations will delight those who enjoy a connection not only to each other but to the outdoors. Those who are more used to having a solid roof over their heads and private bathroom facilities might prefer to ease into the camping experience by sampling one of the Douglas Fir cabins (high $100 range). There are two of these to a building, and each is comfortably equipped with a king-sized bed or two double beds, a fireplace, a skylight, a small refrigerator, a telephone, and a comfortable couch.

For a closer communion with nature, try a Cypress Canvas cabin (mid $100 range), a spartan canvas-sided, canvas-roofed tent with a locking door and sufficient vertical space to stand up straight. These have queen-sized beds with heated pads and safari netting, electric lights, and Adirondack chairs.

The Douglas Fir and Cypress Canvas cabins share camp bathrooms called "comfort stations," which have indoor/outdoor showers with heated floors, a sauna, and a courtyard area with a fireplace. Guests here receive complimentary continental breakfast.

DAYTIME DIVERSIONS

In the **MOTHER LODE**, grab a map and find your way along the twisting back roads to places like **Daffodil Hill**, about three miles north of Volcano, where some three hundred thousand daffodils bloom from mid-March through mid-April.

A **GOLD COUNTRY** visit won't be complete without a stop to a few of the region's many small **wineries. THE SHENANDOAH VALLEY** is home to many, and maps are available from the Amador County Chamber of Commerce in Jackson.

SQUAW VALLEY offers winter activities like **skiing** and **ice skating** in a world-class setting. In the summer, the nearby **Truckee River** between Lake Tahoe's north shore and River Ranch teems with **river rafters**. A beautiful paved **bike trail** also hugs this part of the river.

In **YOSEMITE**, order a couple of deli sandwiches in the village and **rent bicycles** at **Yosemite Lodge**. Pedal along the many paths to a private spot in a meadow for a lunch with a view you'll never forget. The only better vistas, in our opinion, are from **Glacier Point** above Yosemite Valley.

TABLES FOR TWO

At dinnertime in **YOSEMITE VALLEY**, the grand dining room in the **Ahwahnee** is lit with tall, slim tapers placed on each table. Music from a grand piano fills the hall. After dinner, retreat to one of the hotel's cozy public halls for quiet conversation and a warm drink.

Our **GOLD COUNTRY** innkeepers recommend the **St. George Hotel** in **VOLCANO**, the **Upstairs Restaurant** in **JACKSON**, and **Zinfandels** in **SUTTER CREEK**. In **NEVADA CITY**, we were guided to **Friar Tuck's**, **New Moon Cafe**, and **Country Rose**.

In the **NORTH LAKE TAHOE** area, we recommend **PlumpJack Cafe at Squaw Valley** (see listing). In **TAHOE CITY**, dinner at the **Sunnyside** restaurant is served with a shimmering lake view and incredible sunsets. Head for the deck during the warmer summer months. On the south shore, we can recommend **Café Fiore** on Ski Run Boulevard in **SOUTH LAKE TAHOE**.

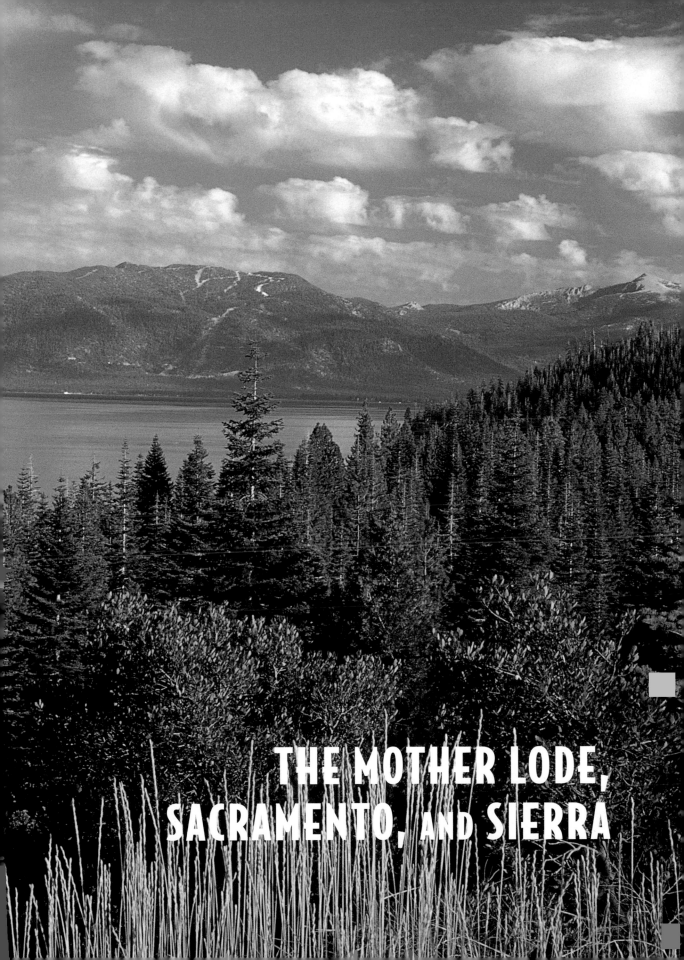

THE MOTHER LODE, SACRAMENTO, and SIERRA

THE FACTS

Seven rooms and suites, each with private bath. Complimentary full breakfast cooked to order and delivered to your room with silver service, or served in gazebo by reservation. Limited disabled access. Two-night minimum for Saturday and holiday stays. Moderate to expensive.

GETTING THERE

The town of Sutter Creek is located on Highway 49, just north of the Highway 88 junction, east of Lodi. The inn is also located on Highway 49, which becomes Sutter Creek's Main Street.

THE FOXES INN OF SUTTER CREEK

77 Main Street
(P.O. Box 159)
Sutter Creek, CA 95685
Telephone: (209) 267-5882;
toll-free: (800) 987-3344
Web site: www.foxesinn.com

THE FOXES INN OF SUTTER CREEK

Unlike some of the Gold Country's other vintage bed-and-breakfast inns, where guests walk on squeaky floors and share old-style bathrooms, The Foxes Inn combines Victorian-style architecture with well-equipped, nicely updated rooms, each retrofitted with its own bathroom. This charming inn also provides a great location in the quaint downtown area of Sutter Creek; shops and restaurants are within easy walking distance.

ROOMS FOR ROMANCE

In the main house, the Honeymoon Suite (high $100 range) is among the inn's plushest love nests. It's a spacious room that contains a canopied queen-sized bed, period furniture, two blue velvet wing chairs, and a sitting area with a fireplace. There's also a very large bathroom with an old-fashioned tub and separate shower. Entry is private, from the porch overlooking the inn's garden.

The Victorian Suite (low $200 range) is a romantic and private second-floor hideaway under skylit eaves. The bedroom has a built-in bookshelf surrounding the fireplace, and there's a separate breakfast room and built-in music system.

The Anniversary Room has been extensively renovated and now has an elegant private bathroom.

Our romantic favorites were some of the rooms found in a separate building behind the main house. The second-floor Garden Room (high $100 range), which overlooks the treetops, is decorated in shades of peach, teal, and cream. Two velvet chairs sit before a wood-burning fireplace. The queen-sized bed is partly canopied and side-draped, covered with a down comforter.

Soft grays and blues complement each other in the spacious upstairs Blue Room (upper $100 range), which features a balcony and private entry. Furnishings include an old-fashioned bathtub and separate shower, a pair of French blue leather wing chairs, and antiques.

The downstairs Hideaway (low $200 range), which boasts a large fireplace, is the inn's largest and most private accommodation.

THE FACTS

Seventeen rooms, each with private bath and air-condition-ing; ten with fireplaces. Complimentary full breakfast served at communal tables. Disabled access. Smoking is allowed on the porches. Most Saturday-night stays require two-night minimum. Moderate.

GETTING THERE

From Highway 99 near Lodi, take Highway 88 to Highway 49; turn left to Sutter Creek. The inn is located in town. From Highway 50 in Sacramento, follow Bradshaw Road south to Jackson Highway (Highway 16). Follow highway east for twenty-eight miles to Highway 49. Follow Highway 49 south for six miles to Sutter Creek. Inn is on right.

SUTTER CREEK INN
75 Main Street
(P.O. Box 385)
Sutter Creek, CA 95685
Telephone: (209) 267-5606
Web site: www.suttercreekinn.com

SUTTER CREEK INN

Sutter Creek Inn and its longtime proprietors, the Way family, are legends in California's bed-and-breakfast industry. When Jane Way bought the old, Greek Revival–style home and opened it to guests some two generations ago, she created one of the West's first bed-and-breakfast inns. Although the industry has since exploded with competition, the inn continues to attract a loyal following.

Since our first visit so many years ago, day-to-day operations have passed to Jane's daughter Lindsay. Lindsay's younger brother David, who has nurtured the grounds for decades, shares management duties. The siblings have worked hard to preserve the ambience that returning guests have grown so fond of, but have freshened the rooms and provided welcome updates as needed.

Although you wouldn't guess it from the street, the gracious property is among the Gold Country's largest inns, with seventeen guest accommodations (all with their own bathrooms). Rooms are located both in the main house and in private outbuildings set among dozens of trees.

ROOMS FOR ROMANCE

A favorite room is the Carriage House, which features a tub for two with a view of the fireplace. It also has a canopied queen-sized bed and a sitting area. The weekend rate is in the mid to upper $100 range.

The Storage Shed (mid to upper $100 range) has one of the inn's legendary swinging beds, which hangs from the cathedral ceiling on chains. You'll be able to see the fireplace from the queen-sized bed, which, by the way, can be stabilized if desired. This room also has a tub for two and a separate shower.

Another queen-sized swinging bed is found in the popular Tool Shed (mid $100 range), which is also equipped with a fireplace and a private patio.

Porch swings behind a wisteria-laden canopy have earned David's Room favored status among returning guests. This elegantly handsome room also has a queen-sized bed, a comfortable couch, and a fireplace.

THE FACTS

Seven rooms, each with private bath; three with tubs big enough for two. Complimentary full breakfast served at communal tables. Complimentary baked goods. Complimentary afternoon wine. Limited disabled access. Two-night minimum stay during weekends and holiday periods. Moderate to expensive.

GETTING THERE

From Interstate 80 in Auburn, take Highway 49 east and drive about forty-five minutes, following signs to Grass Valley. Drive past Grass Valley to Nevada City and exit highway at Broad Street. Turn left and follow to the top of the hill; inn is on left.

THE GRANDMÈRE'S INN

Located on one of Nevada City's historic narrow streets, this three-story Colonial Revival mansion was once the home of United States senator Aaron Sargent, who played a major part in the construction of the transcontinental railroad and who wrote the Nineteenth Amendment giving women the right to vote. His wife, Ellen, championed women's rights with Susan B. Anthony, who was a frequent guest in the home.

Today the impressive property is Nevada City's most romantic inn, treating guests to a helping of history along with present-day comforts. Outside, the inn strikes a prosperous, stately pose, with its wrought-iron fence, mature gardens, and gingerbread flourishes. Inside, the establishment pampers guests with contemporary bathrooms and cushy beds. It's also delightfully free of the antique doily decor that many—especially people of the male persuasion—find off-putting. It's both male- and female-friendly.

ROOMS FOR ROMANCE

One of our favorite romantic retreats is the spacious first-floor Senator's Chambers (low $200 range), which consists of a charming bedroom with a queen-sized bed and a chandelier, and a separate living room with hardwood floors, a fireplace, and a couch. The bathroom has a clawfoot tub and a separate shower. There's also a private porch.

Another large and elegant accommodation is the second-floor Diplomat's Suite (high $100 range), with a queen-sized four-poster bed, a tiny writing desk, and a comfortable sitting area with a pair of wing chairs and a couch. The bathroom contains a deep soaking tub.

Traveling romantics will also enjoy Ellen's Garden Room (high $100 range), which features a separate garden entrance. This cozy and private corner room holds a queen-sized pencil-post bed. The bathroom has an oversized tub and shower.

The inn's least expensive room, offered in the mid $100 range, is George's Room, a front-facing corner room with a log bed.

THE GRANDMÈRE'S INN

449 Broad Street
Nevada City, CA 95959
Telephone: (530) 265-4660
Web site: www.grandmeresinn.com

THE FACTS

Six rooms, each with private bath. Complimentary full gour-met breakfast served by candlelight at communal table or on backyard veranda, weather permitting. Complimentary beer and soft drinks. Two-night minimum stay during most weekends and holiday periods. Moderate.

GETTING THERE

From Interstate 80 in Auburn, follow Highway 49 east past Grass Valley to Nevada City. Take the Broad Street exit. Turn right on Broad Street and make an immediate left on Nevada Street. Inn is on the right.

DEER CREEK INN
116 Nevada Street
Nevada City, CA 95959
Telephone: (530) 265-0363;
toll-free: (800) 655-0363
Web site: www.deercreekinn.com

If you think this Queen Anne Victorian mansion is impressive from the curb, just wait until the two of you check into your room and explore the grounds. One of the more enchanting properties we've discovered in Northern California, the inn sits on a wonderfully lush acre, with a romantic creek running alongside the grounds. Tall trees shade an expansive lawn area with chairs and lounges for the two of you.

Inside, the inn's decor reflects its Victorian heritage. Parlor rooms are richly appointed with antiques, and a formal dining room is the setting for a gourmet breakfast served by candlelight.

Although it's set close to Highway 49, we weren't bothered by traffic noise. In fact, Deer Creek Inn ranks as one of our favorite Nevada County destinations.

ROOMS FOR ROMANCE

Owners Chuck and Elaine Matroni cite the frequency of marriage proposals as one gauge of the romantic potential of the guest rooms. At last count, the leader was Winifred's Room (upper $100 range). The centerpieces of this room are a Waverly-covered queen-sized, canopied iron bed and an in-room clawfoot tub. There's also a romantic love seat and a covered balcony that looks into the trees and over the garden and creek.

Also a romantic favorite is Elaine's Room (high $100 range), decorated in floral patterns and furnished with a canopied iron bed. The bathroom holds a black-and-white-tiled Roman tub with dual showerheads. French doors open to a pair of private patios.

The feminine-style Sheryl's Room (high $100 range) is decorated in peach and gray tones with wicker furnishings and floral accents. A king-sized bed sits in a Queen Anne window. The marble bathroom has a clawfoot tub-and-shower combination. There's also a private balcony.

THE FACTS

Sixty rooms, each with private bath. Swimming pool, two communal spas. Restaurant. Disabled access. Smoking is allowed in some rooms. Three-night minimum stay during holiday periods. Deluxe.

GETTING THERE

From Interstate 80 in Truckee, take the Highway 89 exit and follow the highway toward Tahoe City. Drive ten miles and turn right on Squaw Valley Road. Follow for two miles to the ski area. Inn is on right across the street from the tram.

PLUMPJACK SQUAW VALLEY INN

This upscale Sierra hotel has come a long way since its creation in the 1940s as a no-frills overnight lodge for winter sports enthusiasts. In 1960, it served a stint as a dormitory for delegates to the Olympic Games at Squaw Valley. Renovated in the mid-1990s, PlumpJack Squaw Valley Inn has been transformed into one of the North Lake Tahoe area's nicer small hotels.

The inn is named after Jack Falstaff, a life-loving character from Shakespeare's plays. In keeping with the name, the interior decor, extending from the public rooms to the guest rooms, is theatrical, featuring whimsical metal sculpture and bold architecture. The owners also operate other Northern California Plump-Jack dining and wine establishments.

An especially appropriate destination for couples who enjoy spending time outdoors and savoring the many activities found in the Squaw Valley and north shore areas, the two-story shingled inn couldn't be more conveniently located. It's almost directly under the Squaw Valley gondola that transports visitors to the ski area and to an upper-elevation resort area that includes a year-round ice skating rink. Bicycling and horseback riding are among the warmer-weather pursuits available at Squaw Valley.

The PlumpJack Cafe here is regarded as one of the region's best.

ROOMS FOR ROMANCE

Guest rooms have a contemporary, clean look, and are equipped with king-sized beds or two queen-sized beds. Appointments include videocassette players (there's also a tape library), down comforters, hooded bathrobes, and slippers. Many rooms offer nice mountain views.

Rates from spring through fall are in the high $100 range, jumping to the mid $200 range in the winter. If you're splurging, consider a one-bedroom suite with a spa tub (low $400 range).

Guests have access to a swimming pool and communal whirlpool tubs. At the time of our last visit, the inn offered specially priced romantic getaway/anniversary packages.

PLUMPJACK SQUAW VALLEY INN
1920 Squaw Valley Road
(P.O. Box 2407)
Olympic Valley, CA 96146
Telephone: (530) 583-1576;
toll-free: (800) 323-7666
Web site: www.plumpjack.com

THE FACTS

Ten rooms; all lodge rooms have private baths and gas fire-places. All rooms have a television and videocassette and DVD players. Complimentary full breakfast served at tables for two or more or delivered to cabin rooms. Communal hot tub. Two-night minimum stay for lodge rooms during weekends. Two-night minimum stay at all times for cabins. Three-to-five-night minimum stay during certain holiday periods. Expensive to deluxe.

GETTING THERE

Follow Highway 50 eastbound from Sacramento into the Lake Tahoe area. Turn right at the traffic light on Pioneer Trail, about one-half mile past the point where Highway 89 merges with Highway 50. Drive seven and a half miles to the Ski Run Boulevard traffic light (third light) and turn left. Follow one block to inn on left.

BLACK BEAR INN

With scores of anonymous motels, South Lake Tahoe has never wanted for overnight accommodations. Finding a suitably romantic destination, however, hasn't been as easy. Enter Black Bear Inn, which has emerged as the south shore's most romantic destination.

The inn is impressive from the moment you step through the door. The soaring great room is an architectural work of art, boasting gleaming log beams, a huge river-rock fireplace, expansive windows, and comfortable couches.

ROOMS FOR ROMANCE

There are five wonderful rooms in the main lodge. The most spacious is Sequoia (mid $200 range), where facing love seats are placed at the foot of a king-sized bed.

Most popular is the handsome Fallen Leaf room (mid $200 range), which boasts a corner river-rock fireplace, a vaulted ceiling with exposed log beams, and a small balcony.

For couples seeking a special Tahoe experience, we heartily recommend the freestanding Snowshoe Thompson Cabin (mid $400 range), one of the most romantic mountain accommodations we've ever seen. This luxurious and spacious hideaway features a cozy living room with two chairs and a couch, a dining area, and a kitchenette. A three sided river-rock fireplace separates the living areas from the bedroom. The large bathroom has a separate shower and a spa tub for two placed under a corner window.

The Black Bart and Stagecoach rooms (upper $200 range) comprise the Bonanza Trail Cabin. Each of these rooms has a king-sized bed, a kitchenette, and a river-rock fireplace. The nicely appointed Sutter Cabin has two bedrooms and one bathroom, and makes a good choice for two traveling couples.

BLACK BEAR INN

1202 Ski Run Boulevard
South Lake Tahoe, CA 96150
Telephone: (530) 544-4451;
toll-free: (877) 232-7466
Web site: www.tahoeblackbear.com

THE FACTS

One hundred twenty-three hotel and cottage rooms, each with private bath. Swimming pool, restaurant, tennis court, lounge. Disabled access. Smoking is allowed in some rooms. Deluxe.

GETTING THERE

The hotel is located in Yosemite Valley near the village. From Highway 99 at Merced, follow Highway 140 (Yosemite exit) through Mariposa to the park.

THE AHWAHNEE
Yosemite Village
Yosemite National Park, CA 95389
Telephone: (559) 252-4848
Web site: www.yosemitepark.com

THE AHWAHNEE

If one were to list the man-made wonders of California, Yosemite's grand Ahwahnee hotel would be assured a spot. Its location alone would place it near the top. This magnificent stone and concrete fortress, dwarfed by the gleaming sheer granite cliffs of the Royal Arches, is probably the most dramatically situated (and popular) hotel in all of California.

Five thousand tons of stone were used to build the plush, six-story structure, which opened in 1927. Seven cottages containing twenty-four bedrooms were added the next year. Rates during those early days were $15 to $20 per night.

Although nightly tariffs now start in the low $200 to mid $300 range, the Ahwahnee continues to pack 'em in. Calling even one year in advance still might not guarantee you a room reservation during a peak period.

Set foot in this awe-inspiring hotel and you'll immediately understand why. A timeless Native American theme (combined with some art deco flourishes) permeates the hotel, and the public areas are spacious and inviting. Of particular note is the cavernous dining room with an open-raftered ceiling and peeled, sugar-pine log trusses. More than a dozen floor-to-ceiling windows afford spectacular views. We still recall enjoying a romantic Valentine's Day dinner here years ago while snow fell outside and the sounds of a Steinway echoed through the hall. One of the Ahwahnee's prime attractions is the annual Bracebridge Dinner series, a round of Renaissance Christmas feasts and musical celebrations.

ROOMS FOR ROMANCE

Standard hotel rooms (mid $300 range) are nicely appointed and, depending on location, offer grand views of inspiring landmarks such as Yosemite Falls and Half Dome.

Some of the best views are seen from Junior Suites (mid $400 range), which combine nicely appointed parlor rooms with bedrooms. The El Dorado Diggins Suite boasts a sunken living room, a picture window, and what the hotel describes as Yosemite's only spa tub. Queen Elizabeth and Prince Philip stayed in the Mary Curry Tressider Suite during their 1983 visit.

For a more remote and woodsy experience, many guests prefer the Ahwahnee's upscale cottages (mid $300 range), which offer a romantic charm unique in the valley. Cottages 714 and 719 have fireplaces and king-sized beds. Readers should know that the cottages do not have air-conditioning and can be a wet stroll away from the main hotel building in winter.

THE FACTS

Seventeen rooms, each with private bath and spa tub for two. Chanterelle restaurant. Room service. Disabled access. Moderate to deluxe.

GETTING THERE

Lettered streets intersect numbered streets in easy-to-navigate downtown Sacramento. The hotel is at the intersection of Thirteenth and H Streets.

STERLING HOTEL

Although the capital city region has served as our home base for many years, it's not civic pride that compels us to include Sacramento as a romantic *Weekend for Two* destination. California's capital has more than enough activities and romantic restaurants to keep a traveling couple happily occupied for a weekend away. The city has become especially popular since a certain famous governor took office in 2003.

At the end of the day, there's no better place to stay than the elegant and luxurious Sterling Hotel, situated in a leafy neighborhood in the charming midtown area. With its convenient location, within three blocks of the state capitol, this Victorian-style boutique hotel is popular among visiting business and government types. However, it's also a favorite among twosomes attracted by the hotel's romantic ambience and certain special touches, including oversized spa tubs for two in every room.

ROOMS FOR ROMANCE

On the hotel's second floor, room 202 (mid $200 range) is often requested by couples. It faces the side of the property and is furnished with a beautiful wood-canopied, queen-sized bed that sits before a large window. The spacious bathroom has pink tile and stained-glass windows. A pedestal sink and brass fixtures grace this and each of the other rooms. Each is also furnished with a large deck.

Room 304 is a bright, prominent corner bay room and one of the hotel's most popular. Next door in room 303 (low $200 range), there's a balcony that overlooks magnolia trees in the front. This is a spacious room with Oriental carpet and one of the hotel's largest spa tubs.

THE STERLING HOTEL
1300 H Street
Sacramento, CA 95814
Telephone: (916) 448-1300;
toll-free: (800) 365-7660
Web site: www.sterlinghotel.com

Index

MORE TRAVEL RESOURCES FOR INCURABLE ROMANTICS

Each illustrated with more than 150 color photos, these books by Bill Gleeson are the definitive travel guides to the nation's most romantic destinations.

Weekends for Two books are available from your favorite bookseller or through www.chroniclebooks.com.

FREE WEEKENDS FOR TWO UPDATES

We continue to discover new romantic destinations and reevaluate our currently featured inns and small hotels, and we're happy to share this information with readers. For updates on new discoveries, recommendations, and new books in the *Weekends for Two* series, or to let us know about your experiences, please visit www.billgleeson.com.

FINAL NOTES

No payment was sought or accepted from any establishment in exchange for a listing in this book.

Food, wine, and flowers were often added to photos for styling purposes. Some inns provide such amenities; others do not. Please ask when making a reservation whether these items are complimentary or whether they're provided for an extra charge.

Also, please understand that we cannot guarantee that these properties will maintain furnishings or standards as they existed on our visit, and we very much appreciate hearing from readers if their experience is at variance with our descriptions. Comments from readers of the earlier edition were carefully considered in the creation of this revised book.